WHAT
IS
REVENUE
SHARING
?

WHAT IS REVENUE SHARING ?

CHARLES J. GOETZ

Center for Study of Public Choice
Virginia Polytechnic Institute and State University

THE URBAN INSTITUTE
WASHINGTON, D.C.

The Urban Institute is a nonprofit research organization established in 1968 to study problems of the nation's urban communities. Independent and nonpartisan, the Institute responds to current needs for disinterested analyses and basic information and attempts to facilitate the application of this knowledge. As part of this effort, it cooperates with federal agencies, states, cities, associations of public officials, the academic community, and other sectors of the general public.

The Institute's research findings and a broad range of interpretive viewpoints are published as an educational service. Conclusions expressed in Institute papers are those of the authors and do not necessarily reflect the views of other staff members, officers, or directors of the Institute, or of organizations which provide funds toward support of Institute studies.

Copyright © 1972 by The Urban Institute
ISBN 0-87766-050-6

Library of Congress Catalog Card No. 72-89533

URI-13000 (Refer to this number when ordering.)

UI 108-1200-20   1972

Available from:
Publications Office/The Urban Institute
2100 M Street, N.W. Washington, D.C. 20037

List Price: $1.95

Printed in the United States of America

FOREWORD

This book was written during a period of intense debate on the subject of revenue sharing, and its publication is almost simultaneous with the enactment of legislation which turns revenue sharing into a fact of national political life.

While anticipating the passage of such legislation, the author's aim is not, and has not been, to report on or examine the legislation itself. In the interest of the public discussion that will persist, his goal is to examine what is meant by revenue sharing, to separate and follow some of the often contradictory strands which lead into it, and to spell out important implications which might bear strongly on further legislation and on the manner in which the present legislation is implemented.

Where neither the nature of revenue sharing nor its primary aims have been openly explored and defined, there is fertile ground for rhetoric and special pleading. With legislation that has such potential for reshaping governmental relationships in major and not immediately evident ways, there is consequently a compelling need for dispassionate public analysis of revenue sharing and of the merits and faults of tandem issues which may evolve either legislatively or in interpretation and practice.

The author uses as his framework the legislative history of revenue sharing, beginning in the late fifties when a partial return of federal revenues to state and local governments seemed to some an ideal device for disposing of a federal surplus while simultaneously easing the financial plight of states and cities. Although the surplus was ephemeral and the needs of state and local governments are, on closer examination, not so easily recognized or defined, the impulse toward revenue sharing has persisted for an assortment of reasons. In the mid-sixties, fifty-seven revenue sharing bills were introduced into the Eighty-Ninth Congress. By 1972 the options had been winnowed down to two major proposals —the Mills bill and the Administration bill—but the mood had turned from legislative speculation to legislative decision, thus resulting in the passage of legislation marked by compromise.

This legislative course has been sustained by uneasy agreements between essentially divergent points of view which are not easily disentangled. Since the recently-passed bill blurs the distinction still further, the author pegs his inquiry to the two parent proposals in which the different principles are more clearly isolated, although neither, of course, remain before the Congress. Is the purpose of revenue sharing to augment the role of the states vis-à-vis the federal government, or vice versa? Should the amount each state receives be determined on the basis of its population, the tax revenues it collects, the effort it displays in raising revenues—or should such grants be used to compensate the poorer states for their poverty? If there is to be preferential treatment, who should receive it—rural areas or the cities? What is the most efficient way of making allotments to cities—through state governments, or by direct channels from the federal government?

The compromises incorporated in the enacted bill show that some of the basic questions, though recognized, have not been put to rest. On the contrary, it seems likely

*that questions about fundamental aims and techniques will
revive as the federal legislation is brought down to
practical choices at state and local levels.*

*This book, offered in the interests of fostering further
debate, appraisal, and clarification, is a critical examination
of the many ambiguities which need to be faced.
Commissioned for preparation by the Institute's Studies in
Urban Public Finance under the direction of Harold M.
Hochman, the analysis may offer grist for a number of
mills—whether that of a states' rights conservative, an
income redistributionist, an economist interested in
allocative efficiency, or someone merely interested in how
his own state will fare. The analysis, however, is neutral in
tone, although the author concludes that the more one
considers revenue sharing the less enthusiastic he is likely
to become.*

WILLIAM GORHAM

President, The Urban Institute

October 1972

CONTENTS

WHAT IS REVENUE SHARING?

I
WHAT IS REVENUE SHARING?

"Is it worthwhile?" That, of course, is the ultimate question about revenue sharing. Perhaps the dominant theme of this study, however, is that many of the fundamental issues which underlie that question have not been posed in understandable form. Specifically, the discussion of revenue sharing has been characterized by an extraordinary amount of confusion as to what revenue sharing actually entails in practice and what it is supposed to accomplish. Although the term *revenue sharing*, in its most general sense, has consistently been used to mean a broad form of grant to lower-level governments, the differences among the various specific plans can easily be interpreted as differences of principle rather than of mere administrative details. Moreover, the vagueness and abstraction in the definition of revenue sharing has been nicely complemented by the abstract character of the rhetoric used to justify the plans: "fiscal imbalance," "new federalism," "state-local financial crisis," "first aid to sick governments," etc. As we will see, it is difficult to give these rallying-phrases specific content.

While ambiguity has great appeal in papering over conflicts and inconsistencies, this appeal may be a dubious virtue when a nation faces important decisions about major fiscal institutions. The pervasive ambiguity in much of the debate about revenue sharing is, then, one of the chief reasons for the following discussion.

To relate the general discussion of revenue sharing to the actual political debate, two specific legislative proposals will be given special attention. The 1971 Nixon administration bill illustrates the basic type of legislation which attracted the most attention between 1965 and 1971. The legislation developed by the House Ways and Means Committee in early 1972—hereafter called the Mills bill— represented the most recent major proposal at the time this analysis was undertaken. This latter bill is an extremely complex plan which incorporates some elements of almost every revenue-sharing scheme suggested during the previous decade. Where appropriate, reference will also be made to other specific bills which illustrate notable variations on the two major examples. To some extent, a sharper focus on the specific details of current legislation has deliberately been sacrificed to preserve a broad perspective of the issues which may be of continuing interest during a longer-term debate over revenue sharing and its possible forms and consequences.

PRELIMINARY CONSIDERATIONS

Ironically, the whats and wherefores of revenue sharing are more difficult to disentangle now than ten years ago. Although the recent history of the concept in the U.S. dates to a tax-sharing bill introduced by the then Congressman Melvin Laird in 1958, the idea did not begin to show serious promise of implementation until the early sixties.[1] At that time, two major factors contributed to an explosion of interest in revenue sharing, as evidenced by its active consideration in the presidential campaign of 1964 and the subsequent introduction of fifty-seven tax-sharing bills in the 89th Congress elected that same year. On the one hand,

---

[1] A concise history of the development of revenue sharing since the late fifties may be found in Michael E. Levy and Juan de Torres, *Federal Revenue Sharing with the States* (The Conference Board, Washington, 1970), pp. 8–10.

pressure for new federal spending programs had fallen to an unusually low level—which only hindsight now tells us was to be very temporary indeed—and many were concerned that the vigorous revenue elasticity of the federal tax system would result in potential surpluses whose absorption by new federal programs was doubtful. At the same time, many other informed observers were painting a very dim picture of the ability of state-local revenue systems to generate enough funds to finance the minimum "needs" of the sixties and seventies.

Partisans of almost any political position might, under the circumstances of the early sixties, have agreed on some measure to alleviate the problem of the then-expected emergent federal surpluses and the deflationary "fiscal drag" which they might imply. Viewed in oversimplified ideological terms, however, we may imagine one polar extreme of fiscal conservatives really preferring tax cuts and "less government" as its first choice, while the other extreme of strong public sector activists would ideally have preferred new federal programs. Revenue sharing may be regarded as a "second best" compromise for each of these groups and as a fortuitous occasion to "kill two birds with one stone" by more moderate areas of the political spectrum.[2]

Alas, the waters have been muddied considerably since 1964-1965. Most importantly, the pressure for new large-scale federal-level programs has intensified to a degree which could not have been easily predicted a decade ago. Revenue sharing now competes more directly with such new programs, and the "fiscal dividend" of emerging surpluses no longer looms as an easy source of funding over the foreseeable future. While it is true that governors and mayors still cry in alarm at a supposedly impending fiscal catastrophe, more disinterested specialists now report a far more optimistic prognosis for state-local finances

---

[2] This is consistent with the predictions of the modern theories of political decision making. The basis for the emergence of the median preference position as a dominant policy was described by Duncan Black, *The Theory of Committees and Elections* (Cambridge, 1958), esp. pp. 14–24.

than they did a few years ago. In the context of the seventies, therefore, it is difficult to find in revenue sharing the same simple all-purpose appeal which it enjoyed when it first attracted serious political consideration.

That the conditions of the early sixties have passed does not deny, of course, that they still exercise some residual effect. Public figures do not easily abandon positions which, *carte blanche*, they might find unappealing in the light of present conditions. In general, however, the one-time tactical appeal of revenue sharing should now be supplemented by more substantive arguments.

In attempting to analyze the pros and cons of revenue sharing, there are some areas where one must throw up his hands in despair. One of these is the "opportunity cost" of revenue sharing, the alternative federal programs which might be financed out of the same funds. Argument on this point frequently revolves around specific programs, such as welfare reform, which may be "lost" due to the shrinkage of disposable federal revenue. An alternative way of posing this point is whether federal-type public goods or state-local type public goods represent higher-priority "needs." This is not at all the same issue as whether the federal or the lower levels of government are more effective in ministering to essentially the *same* "needs." Here, one camp trumpets the alleged inefficiency of local government, while the other lauds the "greater responsiveness" of local government in adjusting to a legitimate geographic diversity of preferences. While the former view seems more popular in print, a recent public opinion poll suggests majority support for the latter contention throughout a cross-section of the general public.

Nonetheless, one need not enter the morass of subjective dispute to point out that arguments about the relative productivities of expenditures are to some extent asymmetric. A greater productivity of federal expenditure, for whatever reasons, does imply that revenue sharing should be rejected in favor of retention of the funds by the federal sector. Acceptance of the opposite proposition does not, however, necessarily imply the choice of revenue sharing as opposed to other alternatives, such as federal tax cuts, which would indirectly make more income available for possible use where the electorate finds increased spending by state and local governments more appropriate.

There is more than enough fuel for controversy without belaboring the opportunity-cost aspect of revenue sharing. The remainder of this chapter surveys the major ways in which the principal revenue-sharing plans differ. The successive chapters make frequent reference to the differences between various revenue-sharing formulas, but they are primarily concerned with examining the "why" of revenue sharing, its possible motivations or rationales. Thus, subsequent chapters discuss the efficiency, redistributive, and "new federalism" arguments. "Efficiency" in the sense developed in Chapter II is the economist's technical understanding of the term in reference to conditions which permit costs and benefits to be appropriately reflected in ultimate decisions. Chapter III is in a sense a footnote to the efficiency discussion because it points out some neglected implications of the different revenue-sharing formulas whereby various types of spending and taxing decisions are systematically encouraged or discouraged. Chapter IV provides some state-by-state comparative statistics on the relative sizes of revenue-sharing allotments under some of the basic plans. The impact of revenue sharing on the independence and effectiveness of the individual state government is assessed in Chapter V.

BASIC DIFFERENCES IN REVENUE-SHARING PLANS

While the general public discussion of revenue sharing has often been a case of calling completely different animals by the same name, all of the ambiguities inherent in the general term vanish when formal legislation is prepared. From the outset, the legislative proposals gave varying responses to the two major questions:

(1) What is to be the size of the total revenue-sharing fund?
(2) On what basis is the total fund to be distributed among the recipient units?

Originally, only the states were considered as recipient units. Any "pass through" of grant funds to local governments would have been at the discretion of each state legislature. It has long since become clear, however, that simple political realities dictate a mandatory pass-through of some type in order to reassure urban interests that they will receive a fair share of the funds available within each state. Hence, the basic questions are each separable into two additional subquestions concerning:

(a) the distribution to state governments; and,
(b) the distribution among local governments within each state area.

It is not surprising that proposals about the overall size of the revenue-sharing program have varied widely, ranging from token sums of less than $3 billion to massive grants totalling more than $30 billion. Typically, the alternative programs have been scheduled to rise gradually to their ultimate funding levels over multi-year "phase-in" periods which are designed to cushion the immediate impact on the federal budget itself. Until recently, a consensus appeared to exist that revenue-sharing funds would be linked to some fixed percentage of the federal income tax base. However, the 1972 Mills bill reflects the position that such linkage presents Congress with an "open-ended and uncontrollable" program. The Mills bill, therefore, incorporates a more orthodox set of specific annual appropriations over a fixed five-year period. Nevertheless, without meaning to minimize the importance of any disputes about the method and level of appropriations, one can at least state that the underlying issues concerned are relatively straightforward and easily understood.

The diversity in the distributional formulas which determine the relative shares accorded to different states and local governments has, by contrast, been highly complicated, far more interesting, and of considerably more potential import. While they are often combined or modified in complex fashion, four major distributive principles can be recognized in the various revenue-sharing formulas:

(1) Population
(2) Revenue Effort
(3) Equalization
(4) Federal Tax Collections

Only the latter principle implies true tax sharing in its most narrow sense, since this principle would in effect merely return some proportion of the federal income taxes paid in each state. This "collection" basis does not seem ever to have been viable politically, subject as it was to the criticism of giving the highest per capita grants to high-income states which allegedly "needed" such assistance least.

A straight per capita distribution formula, resulting in grants proportional to a state's population, apparently had the early support of some of the principal proponents of revenue sharing. They argued that population is a reasonably good index of the need for public services and that it enables the grant distribution to allow for varying capacity, since the tax payment *contributions* to the revenue-sharing fund would be higher from the more affluent states. The Pechman task force on revenue sharing, appointed by President Johnson, proposed that the major portion of revenue-sharing funds be distributed to the states on this per capita basis, although the group's report was never made public. In response to a desire to sharpen the urban focus of revenue sharing, the population principle can easily be extended to a single relevant subgroup such as *metropolitan area* population. For instance, urbanized population and total population are given separate and equal weights in part of the distribution formula employed in the Mills bill.

The "effort" principle reflects a desire to "help those who help themselves." In practice, an area's "effort index" has been defined specifically as the percentage of personal income which is extracted by the area's state-local public sector via certain eligible revenue-raising devices. Most of the recent legislation, including the Nixon administration's bill, uses this effort index to adjust upward or downward the recipient government's grant as determined under the straight population formula. Hence, this general type of formula is really a combination of two principles and may be designated the "effort-weighted population" formula. An exception to this general rule is provided by the Mills bill which is based in part upon what can be termed a pure "relative effort" formula, using a recipient's effort index to weigh its *revenue* level rather than its population level. Hence, the administration's type of formula can be regarded as composed of population weighted by relative effort, while the Mills version of a relative effort formula is "pure" in its reliance on absolute effort weighted by relative effort.

One section of the Mills bill also uses what may be termed an "absolute effort" formula which distributes grants in proportion to the revenues raised by local units without any adjustment for income as represented by the so-called effort index. In any event, whether any of the effort indicators basic to these formulations really measure an area's fiscal effort is at least a debatable question. To include an effort element in such formulas does, however, certainly have important effects on the redistributiveness of revenue sharing as well as its incentive effects. These implications are discussed in succeeding chapters.

With the exception of the "collection" basis, all of the

formula variants are implicitly redistributive to some extent. The "equalization" formulas, however, are explicitly redistributive. The major proposals incorporating this principle have used per capita personal income as the key element in the distribution formulas. An area's grant is then designed to vary inversely with its per capita income level. Although this type of explicitly redistributive formula has not seriously been considered as the sole method of distributing revenue-sharing funds, income level has been suggested in several bills as the allocative principle for some fraction of the revenue-sharing fund to be set aside for equalization purposes. The introduction of various poverty indicators, such as welfare loads, into suggested distribution formulas is, of course, also motivated by equalization goals.

It is useful to trace briefly the application of these principles to the two major illustrative bills. Of these, the administration bill is far simpler conceptually. The funds are first divided among "state areas" in accordance with the effort-weighted population formula described above. Then, each state area grant undergoes an intrastate division among the state government and its local governments. Essentially, this latter division is based upon an absolute effort formula, *unadjusted* by any relative "effort index" of the type described above. That is, each government's grant is proportional to its own revenue collections.

The effort-weighted population criterion which plays such an important role in the administration bill introduced in 1971 does not reflect a partisan position. In the same year, the leading Democratic Party figures, Senators Humphrey and Muskie, each introduced revenue-sharing proposals which incorporate essentially the same interstate distribution principle. As noted below, these bills differ from the administration's proposal in a number of other particulars.

In the Mills bill, separate trust funds are established for state governments and for local governments. The local government funds are divided among state areas via a formula giving one-third weight to each of the following:

(1) population;
(2) urbanized population;[3] and,
(3) equalization as reflected in the inverse per capita income principle.

Each state area grant is then broken down to the "county area" level using the same formula. At this stage, things become more complicated. County and township governments receive grants proportional to their shares of all the local government revenues collected in the county area. (This is identical to the intrastate distribution principle employed more extensively in the administration bill.) Finally, the balance of the funds are allocated among the remaining units of general government, giving equal weights to population and inverse per capita income.

The distribution among the states under the Mills bill also follows a complex arrangement. Half of the trust fund is allocated proportionally to a state's use of state individual income taxes, subject to minimum and maximum limits determined by the state's federal income tax collections. Thus, this part of the allocation reflects both absolute effort and collection principles. The other half of the fund is divided among the states according to the pure *relative* effort formula described above.

Although the description of the Mills bill is only a summary one, it should be apparent that this proposed legislation really consists of at least five separable revenue-sharing plans, three applying to local governments and two to state governments. It will be suggested in Chapter IV that the interaction of these many formulas results in mutually counterbalancing effects and an interstate distribution which many may regard as peculiar. Besides being complicated in principle, the bill also presents possible data difficulties with respect to the local government distribu-

---

[3] Urbanized population follows the census definition of residents of any area consisting of a central core of 50,000 or more population and a surrounding closely settled territory.

tions. In particular, annual income and population statistics for small units must be estimated at an undetermined cost and with uncertain accuracy. The simpler formula for intrastate distributions contemplated under the administration bill may represent a concession to practicality and expediency rather than any strong philosophical attachment to the absolute effort criterion.

Almost all of the current bills, including the two major illustrations, do provide some flexibility in allowing the people of a state to agree on alternative methods of intrastate fund distribution. For instance, the Mills bill permits a state legislature to provide that population, weighted by per capita taxes, may be used to replace straight population as an allocative principle for local governments. (This optional formula is, of course, formally identical to a collection-type formula which distributes the grants strictly in proportion to relative revenue levels.[4]) The administration bill permits wider latitude in the form of modifications, but requires that a majority of each of the major classes of government in a state agree to any change.

Besides the distribution formulas themselves, however, several other facets of the various revenue-sharing proposals deserve at least brief mention. An example is the attempt to restrict the use of revenue sharing to certain broad functional areas. For instance, the so-called Javits bill, which was a precursor of the administration bill, attempted to direct revenue-sharing funds exclusively into the fields of health, education, and welfare. Similarly, the Mills bill attempts to ensure that local government grants will be spent only on a set of "high priority expenditures" which includes public safety, environmental protection, public transportation, and sewage and refuse disposal.

These restrictions might have cosmetic advantages in improving the political palatability of the bill, but "money mixes" and it is difficult to imagine how adherence to such

---

[4] When population is multiplied by taxes per capita, population cancels with the identical population figure used in the denominator of the per capita taxes term. Thus, this optional formula really contains only a single variable, the unit's absolute tax level.

broad functional strings could be measured or how a bill containing them could have any real operational impact. It is, of course, possible to require that total expenditures in some specified area must increase by the amount of the revenue-sharing grant. However, even this rule does not take into consideration a normal upward trend and would lose all practical significance over time. In general, restrictions of the type in question have little effect except to place a floor under expenditures in the favored categories. In view of the modest size of any projected grant disbursals, this floor would be so low as to be irrelevant.

By contrast, among the most recent additions to the revenue-sharing package are seemingly minor administrative requirements which may be harbingers of important future developments in the legislation. For instance, in order to maintain eligibility for revenue sharing under the 1971 Humphrey bill, each state's governor would be required to file "a master plan and timetable for modernizing and revitalizing of state and local governments" by methods which the bill suggests via an illustrative checklist. This provision lacks teeth in the sense that there is no procedure to determine whether the required modernization plan is acceptable or not. Thus, no concrete effect can be predicted for this provision in its present form. However, unlike the functional area restrictions discussed above, where the intent is impossible to implement, the Humphrey bill's intent is, with appropriate future introduction of conformance rules, potentially an important and thoroughly enforceable string attached to revenue-sharing monies.

At this point, at least the rough outlines of the most seriously considered proposals should be apparent. The alternative plans reflect principles which vary considerably, both in their philosophical-ideological content and in their actual interstate distribution of the revenue-sharing grants. It remains to be seen whether the different implications of the alternative plans are not perhaps even deeper than superficially appears to be the case.

II
THE EFFICIENCY CASE

Is revenue sharing essentially a game in which funds are merely redistributed among different units and levels of government? That is, does revenue sharing only slice up the fiscal pie in different portions than before? Or, alternatively, does it somehow provide the opportunity for larger slices all around the table?

With certain exceptions, professional economists are usually reluctant to advocate policies on distributional grounds alone and prefer to find a rationale based on genuine net gains or real efficiency rewards from an allocative improvement. Certainly, most of the rhetoric in the revenue-sharing debate suggests that such an efficiency rationale does exist. There are allegations of fiscal "imbalance," "chronic crisis," and "inability to meet the urgent and necessary needs of our citizens." Revenue sharing may then be interpreted as an institutional change designed to correct a recognizable allocative deficiency which in some way arises out of the present set of federal-state-local fiscal institutions in the United States. But what, specifically, is the "deficiency" that should be corrected? [1]

It will not suffice to point to the obvious desire of most citizens for levels of state-local services which far outstrip the levels of revenues now being generated by these governments. There is, after all, always some broad sense in which the "desired" level of state expenditures exceeds the financial resources available. However, this is

---

[1] Much of the material discussed in the following subsections was first presented by the author as, "Block Grants: Medicine for the States' Fiscal Ills?" (Paper presented at the Midwestern Economic Association Meeting, Chicago, Illinois, April 1967).

14

a mere truism which derives from the nonsatiability of human wants, a lack of distinction between *potential* demand and *effective* demand. There is not any problem *ipso facto* when citizens would like to consume more publicly provided goods than they are willing to pay for in their capacities as taxpayer-voters. Some, or even all, of the difficulty in raising state expenditure levels may be simply due to a feeling by the voters that the marginal benefits of state public expenditures do not sufficiently compensate for the marginal tax costs. Our real concern should be directed at possible institutional defects that impede the willingness of taxpayers to support public expenditures whose benefits, under an alternative institutional arrangement, would more than compensate for increased taxes.

EXPENDITURE EXTERNALITIES

When a case for allocative suboptimality must be made, an externalities argument can always be dusted off and brought into play. In this particular case, the premise would be that some state-local expenditures—such as those on education, transportation, and environmental control—have "external effects" in the form of benefits to citizens living beyond the borders of the unit making the expenditure. Rationally, the state-local voters will take into consideration only the internal benefits, i.e., those within their own borders. Thus, the politically effective demand for such expenditures will not fully reflect the overall social benefits, and expenditures will be too low. The traditional remedy for such a situation is some form of grant or subsidy which, by lowering the effective cost of the expenditure, stimulates the activity to its socially optimal level.

This externalities rationale is a bit too facile to be applied to revenue sharing without some critical examination. First, it must be recognized that an argument for federal intervention can be applied only to expenditure categories where the "spillover" externalities transcend state borders. But many expenditures which are externalities for small local governments are substantially internalized within state borders. Secondly, of the remaining externalities which are legitimately interstate in character, many are already dealt with by existing federal grant programs which employ the so-called "matching grant" device to stimulate state-local expenditures in fields which provide externality benefits to the nation as a whole. Moreover, this latter type of categorical grant, preferably broadened in scope as proposed by the "special revenue sharing" plans, is a much more appropriate externality-correcting device than general revenue sharing.

Finally, at least some expenditure categories clearly do *not* provide externalities of any noticeable concern, and general revenue sharing would presumably stimulate these expenditures as well as any other. As noted in Chapter I, broad functional restrictions on the use of funds are ineffective in practice and hence cannot be used as a means of discriminating between externality-producing state-local expenditures and those from which no spillover benefits flow. If one *is* interested in revenue sharing as a corrective subsidy device, there should be a preference for distributional formulas which reduce the cost of state-local expenditures *at the margin* rather than merely inframarginally. From this standpoint, there is a contrast between the effort-based formulas, which do provide an incentive effect and the other principal methods of distribution, none of which reduces the cost of an *additional* dollar's worth of state-local public goods.

If the expenditure externalities argument is to be made at all, it is only fair to raise the counterbalancing argument about externalities on the tax side. "Exporting" of state and local taxes takes place when residents of the taxing jurisdiction do not bear the full burden of the tax. In this case, the taxing unit imposes an external diseconomy, or cost, on the citizens of other units. Since the jurisdiction then faces effective marginal costs which are lower than the true costs, tax exporting tends *ceteris paribus,* to cause higher quantities of publicly-provided goods to be demanded than might be justifiable under social efficiency criteria. In effect, this argument is just the mirror image of the more familiar one about expenditure externalities.

One way in which tax burdens are exported by state-local governments is, of course, by the normal economic process of "shifting" wherein, for instance, a California tax becomes incorporated into the price of oranges paid in New York. But a much more obvious tax-export mechanism is the deductibility of state-local taxes from the federally taxable incomes of both individuals and corporations. This deductibility means, in effect, that a part of each state-local tax dollar really comes out of the federal treasury and not the pocket of the nominal taxpayer. (Local taxes are also deductible from some state income tax bases.) Charles McLure attempted to estimate the total magnitude of this tax-export effect for 1962 and concluded that "services provided by state and local governments may be as much as 15 to 40 percent underpriced."[2]

Externalities, even on the most generous evaluation, do not seem to offer a very compelling case for revenue sharing. On the one hand, unconditional grants seem to be a relatively clumsy tool for subsidizing those activities which may produce spillover benefits. Beyond this, however, one would have to be prepared to argue that the *net* externalities of state-local expenditure, considering those on the supply side as well as the demand side, are positive.

---

[2] Charles McLure, Jr., "The Interstate Exploiting of State and Local Taxes: Estimates for 1962," *National Tax Journal,* 20 (March 1967), pp. 49–77.

SUBJECTIVE COST VARIATIONS

The much higher income elasticity of the federal revenue system has been prominently cited in discussions which suggest that the states occupy an inferior financial position to that of the federal government.[3] This argument was given special attention during the sixties as a justification for revenue sharing. It is difficult to see why so much importance should be attributed to the relationship between the income elasticity of revenues and the income elasticity of desired expenditure. All that this relationship really suggests is that, in a period of secularly rising income, long-run budget-balancing requires either declining, stable, or increasing tax rates according to whether the constant-rate revenue elasticity is higher than, equal to, or lower than the desired expenditure elasticity. The so-called revenue elasticities are, after all, based upon unchanging statutory rate structures and merely tell the amount of *automatic adjustment* in the revenue system. Unless rate changes are, themselves, somehow "costly," tax systems which tend automatically to adjust revenue flows to desired expenditure flows do not possess any inherent advantages over tax systems wherein the same adjustments are performed in a deliberate or discretionary fashion via rate changes.

Are rate changes, then, "costly"? In the strictly objective sense, there is no good evidence to believe that such costs are other than negligible ones, if indeed they exist at all. When, however, the costs in question are defined as subjective costs, the answer may be quite diverse. The "felt" cost of additional taxes may be substantially higher for many individuals when the payment increment is due to a nominal rate increase, than when the same payment increment occurs via automatic adjustment. Fiscal decisions, moreover, are based upon these "felt" or subjec-

---

[3] Formally, the income elasticity of a revenue system is the percent of change in tax collections divided by the percent of change in taxpayer income. Therefore, the more the elasticity value exceeds one, the greater is the tendency for revenues to grow at a faster rate than income.

tive costs, not on the objective cost. Hence, it is plausible that the purely subjective marginal cost for public expenditure financed via revenue-inelastic state taxes is higher than the analogous cost curve for financing via federal taxes. Indeed, this hypothesis seems to be supported by the reluctance of state-local officials to bear the political costs of raising tax rates. Consequently, a shift from the one system of revenue collection to the other may, *ceteris paribus*, "allow" more of the state public expenditure desires of individuals to be willingly financed.

Note, however, that there is an ambiguity here as to which situation really maximizes any individual's welfare, given the true economic relationships which constrain total public and private consumption. There is, seemingly, a "fiscal illusion" which distorts the cost calculus of the individual. But where precisely does it lie? Does the "obviousness" of rate increases in state and local taxes cause the subjective cost of expenditure to be *over*valued relative to the objective cost? Or does the "imperceptibility" of automatic fiscal tax adjustment induce *under*valuations of cost? It is possible that either, or even *both*, of these statements may be true.

Hence, one might be willing to hazard the positivistic or purely explanatory hypothesis that the substitution of federal tax collection for state tax collection will increase the state expenditure level desired by a decisive political coalition. But one should also be extremely cautious in making judgments as to whether such increases would represent improvement or deterioration in the ultimate result. Obviously, this line of reasoning may be rejected by any observer who regards the cost-benefit calculus of the electorate, as exercised through the democratic process, as wrong or irrelevant. Willingness to impose one's own personal value judgments about the "correct" fiscal behavior of state-local governments will suffice to legitimize the manipulation of the electorate's subjective cost as a possible strategic tool to secure the "right" outcome. Nevertheless, such a rationale for revenue sharing, however paternalistic or benevolent it might be, would certainly not bear the slightest resemblance to what is commonly understood as an efficiency argument.

There is another, more clearly negative, aspect of fiscal illusion somewhat allied to the phenomenon just discussed. It is sometimes suggested that federal taxes are regarded by state voters as fixed costs, so that disbursements to a state are viewed by its citizens as "free money" coming at the expense of the federal treasury and not out of state resources at all. This view of federal money can be termed the "Santa Claus Illusion" and is, of course, a case of the fallacy of composition where what seems to be true for *one* of the parts cannot be true when *all* of the parts are considered. Redistributive effects aside, the individual citizen might more appropriately regard revenue sharing as the approximate equivalent of transferring money from one pocket to the other in the same pair of pants.

In sum, the cost illusion factor is absolutely inconclusive as an argument in favor of revenue sharing. While subjective cost considerations might lead one to expect higher state expenditure levels to be induced by what is, in effect, a partially federalized financing system, there is no compelling evidence that such a change would constitute an improvement. Indeed, the opposite argument can quite as easily be made.

TAX-BASE MIGRATION

An efficiency case in the wider sense is suggested by what can be termed a "Sum of the Parts Paradox" applicable to the question of state versus federal financial capacity. One frequently hears that federal financial resources are superior to those of the states. Indeed, this position is implied in the very proposition that the federal government should extend unconditional financial aid to the states. The paradox lies in explaining how the whole, i.e. the federal government, has access to financial resources greater than the sum of those accessible to its fifty parts. After all, the states do have the power legally to impose tax systems which could in all essential respects (except for import-export duties) duplicate that of the federal government. Also, the economic base for such levies is, in the aggregate, almost precisely the same base available to the federal government. How, then, can one reconcile state fiscal "poverty" with what is alleged to be, relatively at least, federal fiscal "affluence"?

What superficially has the appearance of a paradox can be explained by the existence of a Prisoner's Dilemma[4] among the states. Although the aggregate tax base exploitable by the states is (approximately) fixed, any one state is likely to regard its share of this aggregate as a variable. Specifically, the so-called tax-base migration problem is involved here: state and local governments fear that a portion of their economic base will emigrate to lower-tax jurisdictions if their own tax rates get out of line relative to competing geographical locations. This phenomenon has also been described as a case of economic units "voting with their feet."

Supposing, for the moment, that the migration problem is an empirically meaningful one, we can derive something like an efficiency explanation for revenue sharing. In this context, the levying of a tax by any single political

---

[4] For those unfamiliar with the term, the Prisoner's Dilemma is an extremely important game-theoretic concept. It originates from the story of a district attorney who wishes to prosecute two men apprehended in the possession of stolen goods. If they both remain silent, they can expect a one-year term on a stolen goods charge. The district attorney places the men in separate rooms and announces that, if any man turns state's evidence and testifies against his silent accomplice, the "squealer" will go free and the accomplice will receive the heaviest possible larceny charge carrying a five-year term. On the other hand, if both men testify, they will both receive reduced two-year terms. Rational individual choice leads to the prediction that both will "talk" and receive two-year terms rather than the one-year possible through mutual cooperation on silence. Hence, the term Prisoner's Dilemma is used to refer to a broad class of social situations in which rational individual behavior of each group member is inconsistent with the best policy for the group as a whole.

unit may become an external economy-producing activity from the standpoint of other units. For instance, a tax in state *A* may confer a benefit on state *B* to the extent that it occasions a "spill-out" of tax base to state *B*. The standard conclusions of externality theory would then apply in the sense that we would expect the taxes levied by *decentralized* units to fall short of the level where marginal benefits have been equated with true marginal costs.

The Prisoner's Dilemma problem consists of the pressure on each state to "protect" its own tax base by levying only modest rates. However, in the aggregate, this competition cannot change the fixed tax base available to the states, and it simultaneously necessitates foregoing the benefits of expenditure increments. Under these circumstances, the uniform imposition of taxes under centralized federal direction would largely circumvent competitive pressures about relative tax levels. The states can afford to raise taxes *in concert* whereas unilateral action would generate expensive spill-outs.

Of course, the economist will be prompted to attack the above argument on several grounds. In the first place, the evidence for the existence of a strong base-migration effect is poor. Empirical studies of the impact of tax climate on interstate location suggest that taxes are only rarely a decisive factor.[5] To the extent that the migration effect does operate, it will be a more powerful argument in the case of local governments than for states. In fact, it may be argued that for local governments this type of externality can more properly be internalized at the state level than at the federal level. Moreover, the migration argument tends to ignore the expenditure side of the state-local fiscal process: if the marginal benefits of the expenditure are really greater than the costs, increases in taxation might

---

[5] A large number of studies are summarized in J. F. Due, "Studies of State-Local Tax Influences on Location of Industry," *National Tax Journal*, 14 (June 1961), pp. 163–73. However, several studies do indicate sales tax losses to local communities which border on lower-tax jurisdictions: H. G. McAllister, "The Border Tax Problem in Washington," *National Tax Journal*, 14 (December 1961), pp. 326–74; and William Hamovitch, "Sales Taxation: An Analysis of the Effects of Rate Increases in Two Contrasting Cases," *National Tax Journal*, 19 (December 1966), pp. 411–20.

reasonably be expected to prompt a base *influx* in response to the increase in net benefits from the public sector.

It is tempting, then, to dismiss the tax-base migration problem as not a real one. However, this easy answer is comparable to the insensitivity of any medical doctor who would fail to acknowledge that psychosomatic illness, despite its imaginary character, causes real pain and requires real treatment with real medicine.

The fact is that many political decision makers at the state level regard the base migration problem as a very real obstacle to higher taxes. So long as they continue to regard it as a real obstacle, the migration problem has essentially the same effect as if it were a genuine, rather than a psychological, constraint. Whether their "luck" can really be affected or not, many people take pains to avoid walking under ladders. Moreover, the prospects of convincing state officials that their tax climate is of negligible importance is a dim one, since, as in the analogous case of luck and ladders, it is virtually impossible to produce the type of straightforward empirical evidence that would sway a layman with deep-seated preconceptions on the subject. If this line of reasoning, together with all its underlying premises, is accepted fully, one can categorize the state-local financial "ills" as really of "psychosomatic" origin while advocating that the resulting symptoms—suboptimal tax levels—receive real treatment.

None of the revenue-sharing plans can quite be interpreted as federally enforced agreements to raise tax rates despite the fear of a base migration. Although under revenue sharing the state-local unit is, in effect, forced to finance part of its expenditures through the federal income tax, it can still attempt to secure a competitive edge by a compensatory lowering of one of its own taxes. Under the effort-based state area formula and the type of collection-based pass-through formula currently being discussed, there is a penalty for decreasing own-source revenues in this fashion. Alternatively, this may be thought of as an incentive to raise state-local revenues. Strict efficiency criteria then suggest that the strength of the incentive effect be exactly equivalent to the strength of the disincentive effect (if such is believed to exist) of the tax-base migration phobia. The size of the incentive effect is discussed in detail in the following chapter where the reader may judge for himself what size incentive is reasonable in view of the compensatory hypothesis being presented here. Moreover, the tax-export phenomenon should also be considered as an offset to the migration effect.

It is more difficult, but not impossible, to interpret the other basic distribution formulas as an attempt to neutralize migration fears at the state-local level. To do this, one must consider how alternative ways of financing successive budgetary increments might be ranked by a state or local unit's voters in increasing order of burden or cost. These different tax forms or financial media would then be exploited in inverse order of onerousness. For instance, the tax-base migration hypothesis might suggest heavier initial utilization of relatively immobile bases, such as property, turning then, with increasing necessity, to reliance on more mobile bases such as sales and income. Based on this use of increasingly unattractive taxes, it is possible to visualize the relevant marginal cost curve as a "marginal disutility of taxation" which, in conjunction with a "marginal utility of public goods," determines the pivotal median voter's preferred fiscal output for the unit, both as regards taxes and expenditures. Even without any actual monetary effect at the margin, the introduction of a federal block grant may be viewed as shifting the citizen's effective marginal cost curve downward since, at any budgetary level, the marginal financing form is likely to be not as far down the schedule of preferred tax forms. In this case, the state or local unit would not necessarily increase its budget by the full amount of the federal grant, but some increases could be expected in response to what would be perceived as a lowered effective cost.

It may be tempting to attribute to these latter (noneffort-based) grants a positive income effect[6] which partially obviates the argument of the previous paragraph. But, the existence of a noticeable income effect is dubious if we abstract from pure redistributional effects which, because any particular governmental unit could receive either positive or negative redistribution, might work in either direction. This point becomes clear if an opportunity cost of any type—whether it be a tax cut or alternative federal program—is imputed to the revenue-sharing distribution.

TAX-PRICE EQUALIZATION

Although it does not seem to have played any part in popular or congressional discussions of revenue sharing, some of the recent technical literature of economics suggests a rationale for revenue sharing based on the non-neutral interregional effects of public goods pricing.[7] The following summary of the argument is vastly oversimplified, but the general lines of the logic should be apparent.

Suppose that population and the level of public goods provision were basically the same in all regions, but that the income levels of the various communities in these regions varied. As an additional simplifying assumption, let income taxation (or any other tax whose base is positively correlated with income) be the only revenue source of the regional governments. The average tax cost per individual would not vary among the regions, but the average tax *rate* would be higher in the poorer political units. From the

---

[6] "Income effect" is the economist's term for the effect of an increase in wealth, prices being held constant, on an economic unit's demand for goods and services. For "normal" goods, this effect is positive, i.e., generates an increase in the quantity demanded.

[7] This general line of analysis is presented in James M. Buchanan and Richard E. Wagner, "An Efficiency Basis for Federal Fiscal Equalization," in *The Analysis of Public Output* (New York: National Bureau of Economic Research, 1970).

standpoint of strict allocative efficiency there may not seem to be anything necessarily wrong here; it would be equally true that the price of bread, if expressed as a percentage or *rate* of income, would also be higher for poorer people. The problem becomes clear only when one asks where—other things being roughly equal—would a rational person choose to live under these circumstances? Obviously, if one's own income is held constant, it always pays in this simple model to live in the richest possible community, since any other location implies a higher tax rate and, therefore, also a higher money price for the same public goods. In sum, although the price of bread, a private good, is likely to be independent of the incomes of one's neighbors, the price of public goods is not.

While it should now be clear that income levels of communities, acting through local tax rates, may influence residential choice, we still have not pointed out the deadweight allocative loss which may result as a consequence of this. Indeed, if the private sector productivity of an individual were independent of his location, there would be no efficiency loss. More realistically, the advantages of lower tax-price in one area must be seen as counterbalancing factors which may deter individuals from locating where their private sector marginal productivity is highest. Note that, in the oversimplified model which we are deliberately using for clarity's sake, the varying interregional tax prices of public goods do *not* in any way reflect true scarcity values or true differences in the social marginal cost of public goods in different areas. So far as individual location is concerned, the interregional price variations play the role of false signal flags and interfere with the distribution of population according to each individual's maximum productivity.

What the above amounts to, paradoxically enough, is an *efficiency* argument for some form of interregional fiscal *equalization*. Any of the forms of revenue sharing will presumably serve this function to some extent, including the essentially nonredistributive collection-based form of true tax sharing. Of course, the underlying logic of the model becomes much more complex and subject to increasing qualification when it is applied in models which are more nearly descriptive of the real world. Despite these qualifications, and despite its seeming absence in any of the public debate to date, the basic argument stands analytic scrutiny at least as well as the more widely made points discussed above.

THE "ACCOUNTABILITY" DEBATE

As indicated above in connection with the discussion of subjective cost and illusion, fiscal institutions which impede the democratic process in its adjustment to the true preferences of the taxpayer-consumers also create economic inefficiency. An argument *against* revenue sharing has been raised along these lines. Specifically, the fear has been voiced that revenue sharing will reduce the accountability of public officials by breaking the link between the raising and spending of public monies. As a consequence, public preferences would allegedly not be followed and "wasteful" behavior would occur.

While it is impossible to completely refute this charge, neither is it possible to confirm it on the basis of any standard model of competitive political behavior. To the extent that the arguments are not rhetorical, it seems likely that the worry about accountability probably results from a failure to recognize what are really key adjustment variables at the political decision-making margin. It is true that federal monies will enter state-local budgets, but the final decision on the tax load borne by the state-local taxpayer remains in the hands of the same local officials as before. State-local taxes will continue to be the relevant marginal adjustment instruments which elected officials manipulate in the competition to offer more attractive results than their political rivals. On the spending side, it is hard to see how federal grants significantly alter whatever competitive pressure already exists to provide a more attractive spending program than one's opponents.

In sum, the argument presented here is that public officials are not made accountable or unaccountable because of the presence or absence of revenue sharing, but rather because their discretionary behavior must compete with that of alternative candidates who are seeking to win away the voters' approval.

TAX-COLLECTION ECONOMIES

Economies of scale in the tax collection and administration process were once regarded as a strong argument in favor of revenue sharing, but this is now generally recognized as irrelevant. It is probably true that economies of scale are obtainable in tax administration and collection, especially in view of the recent application of computer technology to this field. For the taxpayer himself, moreover, there are compliance costs which are exacerbated by a multiplicity of federal, state, and local taxes. Genuine cost savings may therefore be made possible by a centralization of the tax collection process wherein the federal government acts as an administrator for state and local taxes as well as its own.

To the extent that these considerations apply to revenue sharing at all, they seem to imply the "collection" basis of distribution. However, it is apparent that cooperative collection arrangements can be made quite easily on a voluntary contractual basis, quite apart from the existence of any all-inclusive mandatory plan. Recognition of this fact has resulted in the introduction in Congress of enabling legislation for Internal Revenue Service collection of state taxes on a voluntary, fee basis. Although such provisions have been included as separate titles in several of the major revenue-sharing bills, including the administration and Mills bills, there should be no difficulty in recognizing that revenue sharing and centralized collection economies are quite independent issues.

AN ASSESSMENT

The efficiency analysis of revenue sharing is, in many respects, frustrating: it has something for everyone—but not very much for anyone. There is ammunition for a shaky case on either side, but a solid one for neither. Although it is probable that not much would be gained by introducing greater sophistication, the analysis here has deliberately been presented in relatively simple terms. For this reason, it is perhaps a bit surprising to report that the public political debate has not been couched in similar terms, nor can it easily be translated into such. Hence, it is difficult to say to what extent efficiency considerations either can or do supply a rationale for the current interest in revenue sharing.

III
SYSTEM INCENTIVE EFFECTS

A grant system is "neutral" only when it does not alter the relative attractiveness of options facing the recipient government, i.e., a neutral grant system has no incentive effects. This chapter deals with the possible non-neutral incentives which, either deliberately or inadvertently, may cause certain revenue-sharing formulas to generate changes in the state-local fiscal system.

Grant allocations can, of course, be determined in such a way that their behavioral incentives are nonexistent or negligible. For instance, the revenue-sharing formulas based solely on income and population offer state-local units little or no opportunity to alter their behavior in ways which will increase their grant shares. However, a number of the other formulas under active consideration *do* provide considerable incentives for state and local governments to adopt policies which will increase their revenue-sharing allotments. For instance, any effort-based formula which includes either absolute or relative revenue collection as a variable allows a unit to vary its grant by adjusting the amount of eligible revenue it raises. The strength and mechanics of such revenue incentives will be discussed with particular reference to the Mills revenue-sharing bill and the administration's rival plan. However, it will first be interesting briefly to explore the concept of eligible revenues, i.e., those revenues which count in effort distribution formulas and those which do not.

ELIGIBLE REVENUES

There exists a general agreement that intergovernmental grants and trust fund revenues should be excluded from the effort-based distribution formulas. The remaining so-called "own source" general revenues may be subdivided into "taxes" and "charges and miscellaneous." The principal eligibility issue is whether only taxes should be used in the formulas or whether *all* own-source general revenues, including fees and charges, should count. The decision here is important since it alters the relative distributions among units (as shown by Table 2 in Chapter IV) and also affects the allocation patterns.

To the extent that user charges are practical, they can help to improve the efficient rationing of public goods. Highway tolls, tuition fees, hospital fees, and water and sewerage charges are examples of public services where a pricing mechanism is feasible and usually desirable. To exclude such charges from eligibility would, in effect, encourage state and local governments to substitute taxes for user charges, with possibly undesirable efficiency consequences. Moreover, fees and charges are already discriminated against because, unlike taxes, they cannot be deducted from federally taxable income. At least partially for these reasons, the Nixon administration's revenue-sharing bill therefore includes all own-source general funds in the distributional formulas.

Unfortunately, the arguments here are not completely one-sided. The marginal incentive effects of increasing the eligible revenues can be quite substantial, so that the effective "price" of public goods financed out of such funds is heavily discounted. One outgrowth of this "subsidy" would be to encourage the provision of many services through the public sector when their provision through the private sector would be more efficient. For instance, hospitals and recreation are obvious areas where local governments might feel a strong bias against the private sector in view of the financing advantages obtainable if user charges for such facilities were counted in determining revenue-sharing allotments. State liquor stores are another questionable revenue category. Their inclusion is, oddly enough, permitted in the Muskie bill where eligible revenues are otherwise restricted to taxes. The Mills bill counts only taxes in its distribution formulas, excluding fees, charges, and all types of nontax revenues.

Without hammering the point too heavily, it is possible to describe this eligibility issue as one which does have potential impact on the shape of the future state-local financial system. Unhappily enough, however, the relative merits of the two positions are difficult to assess.

SOME REVENUES ARE MORE ELIGIBLE THAN OTHERS

To paraphrase George Orwell, some revenues are more equal than others. Encouraging the states to substitute income taxes for other tax forms is clearly an objective of some revenue-sharing proposals. Both the Humphrey and Muskie bills, which otherwise resemble the administration plan in their emphasis on an effort-weighted population formula, allow income taxes to be multiplied by two in determining a unit's relative effort index—i.e., income taxes count double. Two incentive effects are really involved here. The obvious and deliberate one causes income taxes to become more attractive relative to other state-local financing alternatives. Less obvious, however, is the approximate doubling of the incentive effect which motivates governments to increase their grant allocations by raising revenue levels. This latter point assumes importance if one wishes to use some of the efficiency rationales presented in the preceding chapter. If incentives are seen as a compensatory effect, then the following seems to be implied regarding the inclusion or rejection of the double-weight procedure: one way is correct and the other is wrong by about fifty percent.

The Mills bill also double-counts income taxes, but not in as straightforward a fashion. Under this bill, two separate distributions are made to state governments, one of which is based principally upon income tax effort and the other on general tax effort. A state's "income tax share" is proportional to 15 percent of its state income tax collections, subject to the limits that this sum be not less than 1 percent nor more than 6 percent of the federal income tax liability attributed to the state. The state's "effort share" is proportional to its tax collections weighted by its relative effort index as described in Chapter I. Unless a state levies a substantial income tax, it fares very poorly in its income tax allotment. Moreover, a dollar of state income tax revenue counts in *both* formulas so long as the state tax generates total revenues between approximately 7 and 40 percent of the federal income taxes collected in the state. Hence, the Mills bill exerts the same two types of incentive effects as the variants of the administration bill which explicitly call for double-counting of income taxes in the distribution formulas.

MAGNITUDE OF THE INCENTIVE EFFECTS

At this point, it should be useful to indicate the approximate strength of these marginal incentives in numerical form. The exact mathematical derivations are provided in the Appendix to this chapter. For each of the revenue-sharing formulas which incorporate a revenue effort variable, we shall report what are, in effect, the number of cents of change in the state's revenue-sharing allotment which would occur if taxes in the state were raised by one dollar. This change in the federal grant can also be interpreted as a percentage "matching grant" or subsidy. Since a number of states have biennial budgetary periods which produce two-year cycles in their revenue system adjustment, the data used are averaged for the two-year period 1969–1970. Of course, these and the other estimates presented in Chapter III are merely illustrations based on historical data and need not reflect the future in anything more than an approximate manner.

In interpreting the figures, two things should be borne in mind. First, the revenue-sharing formula may permit a recipient to alter its *share* of the federal funds, but the *total* distribution to all units is typically a fixed sum. The incentive effect exists when a single unit adjusts its revenues subject to some fixed assumption as to what revenue efforts will be made by other governments. However, it is obviously possible for all governments to adjust their efforts upward equiproportionally, so that not a single unit is actually successful in increasing its grant. Thus, effort competition places the state-local governments in the dilemma of a fixed-sum game.[1]

Secondly, since the formulas determine only *shares*, the translation of a share change into a dollar amount depends critically on the total sum in the fund being allocated. Thus, the marginal incentives generated by a revenue-sharing fund of $10 billion are exactly ten times as strong as when the fund is only $1 billion. Because the dollar amounts vary in each specific bill and, indeed, even from year-to-year, we try to make the impacts of different formulas comparable by reporting the incentive effect *per billion dollars* in the relevant fund. Hence, the reader may calculate the actual magnitudes by multiplying the num-

---

[1] "Fixed-sum game" is the game theorist's term for a situation where the total sum of the benefits to a group of participants is fixed. One participant cannot gain unless one or more other participants suffers an exactly counterbalancing loss.

bers in the tables by the number of billions to be allocated via any particular formula.

The first column of Table 1 shows the percentage matching grant which would be present under the Nixon administration bill. As the Appendix shows, the local governments within a state area would enjoy rates slightly higher than these, but the difference is negligible, amounting to no more than one one-hundredth of one percent. These incentive effectives are closely related to per capita state income, the lowest income states having the highest incentive rates. Since the computations are based exactly on the administration bill, which does not double-count income taxes, most of the column one figures would have to be almost doubled if income taxes were treated preferentially and if the government in question were altering income tax revenues.

The second column of Table 1 shows the incentive effect applicable to the Mills plan's "tax effort share" which is distributed to state governments. An *asterisk* next to this figure indicates that the state also levies an income tax which lies in the effective marginal subsidy range of the "income tax share" formula of the Mills bill. Under present circumstances, a state in this range can gain an additional 7½ cents of revenue-sharing funds for every $1 it raises in new income tax revenues. Since the same income tax revenues count in both the tax effort and income tax share formulas, these effects are additive and raise the combined subsidy rate to almost 10 percent for some states, even when only $1 billion is distributed via the tax effort formula.

TABLE 1   PERCENTAGE MARGINAL SUBSIDY EFFECTS PER $1 BILLION DISTRIBUTED (1969-70 Average)

	Administration Bill's Formula	*Mills Bill's "Effort Share" Formula*
ALABAMA	1.34	1.99
ALASKA	0.85	2.00*
ARIZONA	1.11	2.60
ARKANSAS	1.38	2.01
CALIFORNIA	0.82	2.40
COLORADO	1.04	2.42
CONNECTICUT	0.79	2.06
DELAWARE	0.90	2.19*
FLORIDA	1.07	2.07
GEORGIA	1.15	2.02
HAWAII	0.89	2.84*
IDAHO	1.21	2.45*
ILLINOIS	0.83	2.09
INDIANA	1.00	2.05
IOWA	1.03	2.54
KANSAS	1.00	2.24
KENTUCKY	1.25	2.18
LOUISIANA	1.24	2.40
MAINE	1.19	2.45*
MARYLAND	0.91	2.36
MASSACHUSETTS	0.89	2.43
MICHIGAN	0.91	2.34
MINNESOTA	1.01	2.51
MISSISSIPPI	1.49	2.51
MISSOURI	1.04	2.00
MONTANA	1.15	2.59*
NEBRASKA	1.03	2.31
NEVADA	0.86	2.44*
NEW HAMPSHIRE	1.08	2.01*
NEW JERSEY	0.84	2.10
NEW MEXICO	1.25	2.55*

(continued)

---

* See text, p. 34.

Table 1 continued

	Administration Bill's Formula	Mills Bill's "Effort Share" Formula
NEW YORK	0.77	2.50
NORTH CAROLINA	1.19	2.07
NORTH DAKOTA	1.25	2.68*
OHIO	0.95	1.84
OKLAHOMA	1.16	2.09
OREGON	1.04	2.41
PENNSYLVANIA	0.96	2.10
RHODE ISLAND	0.97	2.28
SOUTH CAROLINA	1.31	2.02
SOUTH DAKOTA	1.21	2.73*
TENNESSEE	1.25	2.01
TEXAS	1.08	1.90
UTAH	1.23	2.54*
VERMONT	1.13	2.86*
VIRGINIA	1.06	2.10
WASHINGTON	0.94	2.41
WEST VIRGINIA	1.29	2.25
WISCONSIN	1.03	2.83
WYOMING	1.11	2.77*
DISTRICT OF COLUMBIA	0.87	2.53*

Because of the relatively low level of the distribution process at which the effort variables come into play, the Mills bill's local government revenue-sharing fund does not generate significant incentive effects. The county government's share of the county area allotment does depend on the ratio of its revenues to the total tax revenues in the county area. But, since the county area allotment is itself rather modest in size, even a relatively large *share* increment does not translate into significant dollar terms. An option in the Mills bill permits state legislatures to substitute the effort-weighted population formula for straight population as one of the three principles which determine the distribution of local grants within a state. However, even the use of this option does not lift the effects out of the negligible range.

While the class of revenue-sharing proposals exemplified by the administration bill exerts approximately equal marginal subsidy effects through state taxes and local taxes, the Mills bill provides effective marginal subsidy rates only on state taxes. This suggests that rational voters might, therefore, increase their reliance on state financing rather than local tax financing.

For equal amounts of money, the Mills formulas seem to be:

(1) more stimulative; and,
(2) less discriminatory among states.

However, the Mills plan allots only the state government portion of revenue sharing through the formulas in question, while the Nixon administration bill channels the entire revenue-sharing fund through effort formulas. Thus, an illustration of the actual magnitudes contemplated in the bills would require applying a multiple of five to the administration figures and of only one to the Mills figures in order to reflect the approximate number of billions involved.

Actually, the Table 1 figures are less interesting for estimating the effects of current legislation than they are for projecting possible future effects if revenue sharing should ultimately be funded at much higher levels and become a really major source of state-local finances. As the program grew into the tens of billions of dollars, the degree of subsidy would increase proportionately so that an increasingly large fraction of the marginal cost of nonfederal public goods would be defrayed by revenue sharing. Note that revenue sharing, by operating on marginal costs, need not even amount to any large fraction of total state-local expenditures in order to exercise this powerful "price effect."

Especially when taken in conjunction with the existing impact of the state-local tax deductibility privilege, revenue sharing presents a clear danger of generating greatly excessive incentive effects even if one fully accepts one or more of the revenue-sharing arguments which justify some degree of stimulus. Besides discriminating against all private sector goods, the marginal subsidies to the state-local sector would also distort voters' abilities to assess the relative merits of federal versus state-local provision of government services.

Finally, an interesting variation on the effort-based formulas is the use of a "benchmark" effort variable. Rather than apply a state's normal effort index as a weight in the formula, only the excess of the effort index over the benchmark is used.[2] This vastly increases the marginal incentive effects, as one can easily see if he reflects that a state whose effort exceeds the benchmark by, say, only one percentage point can almost double its entitlement by raising its effort index an additional percentage point.

NON-NEUTRAL FEATURES OF LOCAL GOVERNMENT ALLOTMENT FORMULAS

The eligibility of different types of revenue has already been discussed, but that of political units has not. Mandatory pass-through in the administration bill and a completely separate local government fund in the Mills bill are devices to insure the eligibility of local units, rather than leave this to the discretion of the states. Both the administration's proposal and the Mills plan qualify as relatively neutral, treating all *general purpose* governments (counties, cities, and townships) on an equal foot-

---

[2] This modification was proposed in a plan devised by the National League of Cities in the late sixties.

ing. Even in this legislation, however, special districts are excluded. This exclusion implies that, other things being equal, a community which finances services such as education, recreation, or sanitation through independent districts or special authorities would be disadvantaged in comparison to one which does not. Thus, one would expect this provision to reduce the importance of special districts as a mode of supplying local government services. While it has been widely noted that the special district form has frequently been abused and overused, the general case here is not completely one-sided.

Other bills whose interstate formulas are similar to that of the administration proposal, use pass-through formulas which go a step further in discriminating among local units, particularly on a size basis. For example, units under some cut-off point (e.g., 25,000) are completely excluded, while those over 100,000 are given a double share in the local government funds. At least two purposes are involved here:

(1) to sharpen the "urban problem" focus of the revenue-sharing distributions; and,

(2) to promote local government structural reform by penalizing what are allegedly "non-viable" or "inefficient" small governments.

The Mills bill accomplishes a similar type of size discrimination by giving "urbanized population" (cities of 50,000 or more plus surrounding closely-settled area) one-third of the weight in determining local government grants down to the county area level. While the proposition regarding efficient size is difficult to confirm with objective empirical evidence, it does command some widespread support. There may, however, be a corollary implication that *excessive* size should also be penalized in the distribution formulas. In the light of some recent theoretical work on the thesis of urban overconcentration,[3] a subsidy to a large metropolis may actually be viewed as counterproductive to the extent that it encourages still further in-migration. Strengthening smaller governments may have a greater effect in alleviating the "urban problem" than direct expenditure in the large cities. By this hypothesis, it is the medium-sized cities which should be most favorably treated, while *both* size extremes should be discriminated against.

HOW MUCH NON-NEUTRALITY?

We have suggested that specific provisions in those distribution formulas which are currently most popular put pressures on the choice of state-local fiscal instruments, the levels of the budget, and the sizes and functional organizations of state-local units. This is not to suggest that some non-neutrality is necessarily a bad thing. Quite the contrary, non-neutrality is essential when an existing misallocation must be corrected. Non-neutralities should, then, be judged against two questions. If an instrument to increase incentives is needed at all, does the instrument in question unambiguously move things in the right direction? If so, can the strength of the incentive effect be properly measured to avoid creating a misallocation in the opposite direction? Also, of course, provisions which have been proposed or adopted primarily for their distributional effects should be examined for possibly unintended allocative implications.

---

[3] Among the relevant studies are: J. M. Buchanan and R. E. Wagner, "An Efficiency Basis for Fiscal Equalization," in *The Analysis of Public Output*, ed. by J. Margolis (New York: National Bureau of Economic Research, 1970); C. J. Goetz, "Fiscal Incentives for the Cities," paper prepared for the Committee on Urban Public Economics, 1970 (mimeographed); J. M. Buchanan and C. J. Goetz, "Efficiency Limits of Fiscal Mobility: An Assessment of the Tiebout Model," *Journal of Public Economics*, I (April 1972).

APPENDIX

Marginal Incentive Effect Derivations

For those interested in the technical aspects of the incentive effects, the general method of their derivation is outlined below. The administration bill is treated first, since the derivation of its incentive effects is more complicated than for the Mills bill.

ADMINISTRATION BILL

Let R_j be the eligible revenues of any government j in the state area to which government i belongs. The total eligible revenues of the n governments in i's state area are

(1)

$$T_i = \sum_{j=1}^{n} R_j .$$

Using α to denote the *inverse* of per capita personal income in any state area k, we define an exogenous variable[4] C_i which reflects the revenue activities in all state areas other than the one to which government i belongs:

$$(2) \qquad C_i = \sum_{k=1}^{51} \alpha_k T_k - \alpha_i T_i .$$

Then the fraction A_i of the national fund allocation to i's *state area* entitlement is

$$(3) \qquad A_i = \frac{\alpha_i T_i}{(C_i + \alpha_i T_i)} .$$

Under the collection-based pass-through formula, unit i's share S_i of its relevant state area funds will be

$$(4) \qquad S_i = \frac{R_i}{T_i} .$$

---

[4] It is assumed that any single state treats this as an externally determined parameter or expectation, much as competitive firms treat the behavior of other firms in the large-number setting.

Finally, if the size of the national revenue-sharing fund is K, i's dollar entitlement G_i is determined by the formula

(5)
$$G_i = S_i \cdot A_i \cdot K.$$

The change in unit i's revenue-sharing grant produced by a marginal change in i's own revenue is

(6)

$$\frac{\partial G_i}{\partial R_i} = \left[S_i \frac{\partial A_i}{\partial R_i} + A_i \frac{\partial S_i}{\partial R_i} \right] K.$$

The first term in the brackets is the "positive-sum" effect which increases i's allotment along with all other units in the state. The second term is the "zero-sum" or strictly competitive effect whereby i increases his share of the state area grant at the expense of other units. Also, it is important to note that the size of the effect is a direct multiplicative factor of the size of the national fund K.

The explicit form of (6) is

(6a)

$$\frac{\partial G_i}{\partial R_i} = \left[\frac{aR_iC_i}{T_i(C_i+\alpha T_i)^2} \quad \frac{\alpha\left(1-\frac{R_i}{T_i}\right)}{C_i+\alpha T_i} \right] K$$

and this formula has been used to calculate state government and local government incentive effects.[5] The change in the state area allocation when any government in the state area adjusts its revenues is

(7)
$$\frac{\partial A}{\partial T_i} \cdot \frac{\alpha C_i}{(C_i+\alpha T_i)^2}.$$

---

[5] Results of this type were first computed in C. J. Goetz, "Federal Block Grants and the Reactivity Problem," *Southern Economic Journal*, XXXIV (July 1967). An updating, to reflect new pass-through provisions, was attempted in D. Johnson and C. Mohan, "Revenue Sharing and the Supply of Public Goods," *National Tax Journal*, XXIV (June 1971). However, Johnson and Mohan give misleading estimates of the local government incentive since, unlike formula (6a), their derivation employs simplifying assumptions which modify the results.

It is of some interest to note the influence exerted by a government's relative size in its relevant state-local sector. Let this be measured by

(8)
$$Z_i = \frac{R_i}{T_i}.$$

Taking the appropriate cross-partial, we have

(9)

$$\frac{\partial G}{\partial R_i \, \partial Z} = \alpha K \left[\left(\frac{c_i}{(c_i + \alpha T_i)(c_i + \alpha T_i)} \right) - \frac{1}{(c_i + \alpha T_i)} \right]$$

whose value must always be negative because of the bracketed term. Hence, other things being equal, a larger unit (in terms of revenue collection) has a lower incentive effect than a smaller one in the same state. In practice, however, these size effects are very small and the figures cited in Table 1 are good approximations for all governments in the state area.

MILLS BILL

State governments are affected by incentive effects under the Mills plan's tax effort distributions. Let T_i be defined as in (1) above as the total revenues in a state area and consider i as the state government. Let β signify the inverse of the state's personal income

(10)
$$\beta_i = \frac{1}{Y_i}$$

and Q_i be defined analogously to C_i in (2) above

(11)
$$Q = \sum_{k=1}^{51} T_k^2 \beta_k - T_i^2 \beta_i$$

so that the ith state government's share S_i of the effort fund under the Mills plan may be written as

(12)
$$S_i^* = \frac{T_i^2 \beta_i}{Q_i + T_i^2 \beta_i}$$

and the rate of change in this share represented by the derivative

(13)
$$\frac{\partial S_i^*}{\partial T_i} = 2T_i \beta_i (1 - S_i^*).$$

The rate of change in the *grant* is, then, this quantity multiplied by the amount being distributed K^*. The Table 1 effects of the Mills plan are based on this computation. These incentives affect state governments only.

If the previous derivations are understood, then it can be seen why the incentive effects due to the Mills plan's local government distributions are negligible. The reason is that, unlike the administration bill, the state area distributions cannot themselves be affected by the behavior of lower level governments. Therefore, local governments are competing for a share of a (relatively) small sum. Even if the *rate* of share change, analogous to (13) above, were quite large, the multiplication by a small value of K does not allow the share change to be translated into a significant grant change. The same reasoning, of course, is doubly appropriate when applied to the even lower-level distribution of county area grant funds.

IV
DISTRIBUTION ASPECTS OF REVENUE SHARING

A desire to incorporate equalization or redistributional elements into the revenue-sharing concept has been apparent in both the political and academic considerations of revenue sharing. Here, the analyst enters the realm of value judgment and cannot say whether the degree of redistribution under a particular proposal "errs" in one direction or the other, or is "just right." Nonetheless, the distributive implications of the various alternatives do differ and some purely factual information on these differences is valuable in forming one's personal judgments.

SOME ILLUSTRATIVE RESULTS

Table 2 presents state-by-state results under representative forms of the major distributional formulas. Column 1 lists the per capita grant to a state area, per $1 billion in the revenue-sharing fund, assuming that allotments are distributed on the collection-based principle. The succes- sive columns indicate the effects of alternative formulas on the per capita state grant. These latter results are in the form of "redistribution ratios" which represent the ratio of the grant in question to the same state's grant under the collection-based plan.[1] This redistribution ratio is sug-

---

[1] The redistribution ratio for the collection principle is not listed since it is, of course, exactly 1.0 by definition for each state.

gested as an approximate measure of the interstate redistribution involved, since it compares a state's share of the input into the revenue-sharing fund (through the federal income tax) to its share of the receipts. A ratio of 1.25 may be interpreted as indicating that a state gets back $1.25 for every $1.00 it has contributed, through federal income taxes, to the revenue-sharing funds.

The per capita grant per $1 billion of revenue-sharing funds distributed under any particular principle may be computed by multiplying the collection-based grant by the appropriate redistribution ratio. For instance, if column 1 is $4.00 and the redistribution ratio for the straight population principle is 1.25, then the state's per capita population-based grant would be $4.00 × 1.25 = $5.00 for every billion dollars distributed by the federal government via this formula. The per capita grants are more informative than total figures for each state, since the state totals are overwhelmingly influenced by state size. Besides adjusting for this state-size bias, the per capita grants allow one to get some feel for the relatively small amounts of taxpayer relief involved. For instance, a $10 billion total revenue-sharing fund involves multiplying column 1 by a factor of ten, but this would generate an interstate average of only about $50 per person.

In computing Table 2, average results for the two-year period 1969–70 are utilized to minimize the influence of biennial state budget cycles. Obviously, however, the particular figures for individual states are sensitive to year-to-year changes, especially major changes in revenue systems.

TABLE 2   DEGREES OF REDISTRIBUTION UNDER ALTERNATIVE REVENUE-SHARING FORMULAS (1969-70 Average Results)

	Grant	Redistribution Ratios for Alternative Formulas							
	(1)	(2)	(3)	(4)	(5)	(6)	(7)	(8)	(9)
	$ per capita Coll.-Based Grant	Straight Popu-lation	Urban Popu-lation	Inverse Income	Overall Mills Local Govt. For-mula	Effort-Weight-ed Pop. (Admin-istra-tion Bill)	Mills Effort For-mula	State Income Tax Incen-tive	Overall Mills State Govt. For-mula
ALABAMA	2.98	1.65	1.06	2.21	1.64	1.58	0.83	0.77	0.80
ALASKA	5.07	0.98	0.00	0.82	0.60	3.27	0.77	2.14	1.45
ARIZONA	3.82	1.29	1.42	1.42	1.37	1.44	1.34	0.90	1.12
ARKANSAS	2.67	1.84	0.63	2.53	1.67	1.67	0.91	0.76	0.83
CALIFORNIA	5.46	0.90	1.25	0.77	0.98	1.06	1.41	0.99	1.20
COLORADO	4.23	1.16	1.28	1.20	1.21	1.24	1.12	1.29	1.21
CONNECTICUT	7.85	0.63	0.75	0.49	0.62	0.52	0.58	0.48	0.53
DELAWARE	6.28	0.78	0.85	0.70	0.78	0.79	0.71	1.90	1.31
FLORIDA	4.36	1.13	1.17	1.21	1.17	1.06	0.79	0.48	0.64
GEORGIA	3.71	1.33	0.93	1.52	1.26	1.23	0.81	0.97	0.89
HAWAII	5.09	0.97	0.96	0.85	0.92	1.13	1.50	2.52	2.01
IDAHO	3.13	1.57	0.21	1.88	1.22	1.68	1.33	1.86	1.59
ILLINOIS	6.43	0.77	0.93	0.65	0.78	0.66	0.74	0.84	0.79
INDIANA	4.79	1.03	0.81	1.03	0.96	0.92	0.75	0.78	0.76
IOWA	4.01	1.23	0.63	1.26	1.04	1.33	1.31	0.90	1.11
KANSAS	4.14	1.19	0.72	1.18	1.03	1.18	1.02	0.77	0.90
KENTUCKY	3.23	1.53	0.91	1.91	1.45	1.48	0.98	1.09	1.04
LOUISIANA	3.39	1.45	1.17	1.81	1.48	1.66	1.15	0.48	0.82
MAINE	3.64	1.35	0.40	1.59	1.12	1.32	1.16	0.53	0.84
MARYLAND	6.06	0.81	0.92	0.74	0.82	0.80	0.87	1.55	1.21
MASSACHUSETTS	5.76	0.85	1.12	0.76	0.91	0.83	1.02	1.48	1.25
MICHIGAN	5.61	0.88	0.96	0.81	0.88	0.92	0.97	0.80	0.88
MINNESOTA	4.20	1.17	1.00	1.19	1.12	1.31	1.27	1.99	1.63
MISSISSIPPI	2.18	2.26	0.57	3.35	2.06	2.56	1.62	0.84	1.23
MISSOURI	4.53	1.09	1.02	1.13	1.08	0.93	0.72	0.57	0.64
MONTANA	3.40	1.46	0.51	1.65	1.20	1.62	1.43	1.53	1.48

(continued)

Table 2 continued

	Grant	Redistribution Ratios for Alternative Formulas							
	(1)	*(2)*	*(3)*	*(4)*	*(5)*	*(6)*	*(7)*	*(8)*	*(9)*
	$ per capita Coll.- Based Grant	*Straight Popu- lation*	*Urban Popu- lation*	*Inverse Income*	*Overall Mills Local Govt. For- mula*	*Effort- Weight- ed Pop. (Admin- istra- tion Bill)*	*Mills Effort For- mula*	*State Income Tax Incen- tive*	*Overall Mills State Govt. For- mula*
NEBRASKA	3.93	1.25	0.85	1.28	1.13	1.30	1.11	0.75	0.93
NEVADA	6.72	0.73	0.85	0.62	0.74	0.81	0.86	0.48	0.67
NEW HAMPSHIRE	4.51	1.09	0.44	1.17	0.90	0.91	0.69	0.48	0.59
NEW JERSEY	6.26	0.79	1.14	0.66	0.86	0.68	0.74	0.48	0.61
NEW MEXICO	3.10	1.59	0.80	1.97	1.45	1.99	1.40	1.01	1.20
NEW YORK	6.49	0.76	1.02	0.61	0.80	0.91	1.43	1.90	1.67
NORTH CAROLINA	3.36	1.47	0.60	1.75	1.27	1.31	0.91	1.50	1.21
NORTH DAKOTA	2.74	1.81	0.27	2.23	1.43	2.45	1.75	0.85	1.30
OHIO	5.37	0.92	0.98	0.88	0.92	0.75	0.58	0.48	0.53
OKLAHOMA	3.54	1.39	0.98	1.61	1.33	1.38	0.88	0.56	0.72
OREGON	4.42	1.11	0.89	1.16	1.05	1.20	1.06	2.10	1.58
PENNSYLVANIA	5.08	0.97	0.98	0.94	0.96	0.85	0.81	0.48	0.64
RHODE ISLAND	5.01	0.98	1.34	0.95	1.09	0.89	0.89	0.53	0.71
SOUTH CAROLINA	2.93	1.68	0.73	2.19	1.53	1.48	0.89	1.21	0.55
SOUTH DAKOTA	2.80	1.76	0.34	2.11	1.41	2.09	1.83	0.48	1.16
TENNESSEE	3.60	1.37	0.89	1.70	1.32	1.21	0.76	0.48	0.62
TEXAS	4.26	1.16	1.22	1.26	1.21	1.01	0.68	0.48	0.58
UTAH	3.20	1.54	1.79	1.88	1.74	1.70	1.36	1.59	1.48
VERMONT	3.81	1.29	0.00	1.88	1.74	1.47	1.59	2.26	1.92
VIRGINIA	4.39	1.12	1.00	1.19	1.10	1.00	0.80	1.30	1.05
WASHINGTON	5.28	0.93	0.88	0.88	0.90	1.02	0.99	0.48	0.74
WEST VIRGINIA	3.48	1.41	0.48	1.81	1.23	1.36	0.95	0.73	0.84
WISCONSIN	4.43	1.11	0.89	1.15	1.05	1.31	1.53	2.27	1.90
WYOMING	4.00	1.23	0.00	1.35	0.86	1.70	1.43	0.48	0.96
DISTRICT OF COLUMBIA	5.90	0.83	1.43	0.72	0.99	0.81	1.04	0.48	0.76

The principles underlying columns 2, 3, and 4 are those used in the Mills bill to determine the interstate distribution of funds for local governments. Straight population and urban population require no additional explanation, since the grants are simply allotted in direct proportion to a state's share of these national population measures. The equalization-weighted population grant is slightly more complicated, however. Under this formula, the state area's straight population grant is adjusted upward or downward to reflect the extent to which the state's per capita income diverges from the national average.[2] This particular formula is actually less extreme than similar plans which appeared in some earlier bills and proposals. These latter types of equalization formulas typically achieved greater

---

[2] The exact formula used is:

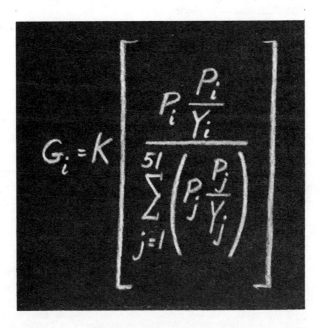

$$G_i = K \left[\frac{P_i \dfrac{P_i}{Y_i}}{\displaystyle\sum_{j=1}^{51} \left(P_j \dfrac{P_j}{Y_j} \right)} \right]$$

where G_1 is the state area grant, and P and Y represent state population and state personal income, respectively. The size of the total revenue-sharing fund to be distributed under this formula is K.

redistribution by limiting participation to some particular selection (or subset) composed of low-income states only.

In the first equalization plans of this type, the subset was limited to a specified fraction, ranging from one-fourth to one-half, of the states, with eligibility determined in the order of lowest per capita state incomes. However, this introduced a discontinuity in the disbursements as small variations in the incomes of the marginally eligible (or ineligible) states would cause such borderline states to rotate in and out of the plan from year to year. This problem may be mitigated by defining eligibility in terms of a benchmark level, such as the national average of per capita income. States exceeding this level would receive no equalization grants. In this case, the number of eligible states would vary from year to year and a state's grant would gradually phase out as its income level approached the national average.

Column 5 of Table 2 is merely an average of the previous three columns, since the Mills bill gives equal weight to each of these principles in determining the funds to be distributed to local governments. Such weighted combinations of distribution principles often give surprising results. In this case, the distributional impacts of the urban population and equalization principles tend to be mutually counterbalancing, since urbanized states generally have relatively high per capita incomes. As a consequence, the Mills grants to local government have an average deviation from the straight population basis of only about 5.5 percent.[3] (See Table 3.) In view of the relative unpopularity of the straight population principle, this result may be surprising.

Column 6 of Table 2 shows the results under the effort-weighted population formula which determines interstate distributions under the 1971 administration bill and which

[3] This result was first pointed out, using different data, by Stephen Dresch in "Assessing the Differential Regional Consequences of Federal Tax-Transfer Policy" (April, 1972; mimeographed), a paper presented to the Regional Economic Development Research Conference and Workshop. Dresch's paper also contains a wider discussion of issues germane to this chapter.

commanded the heaviest support during the late sixties.[4] As noted in earlier chapters, the two most common variations on this formula involve: (1) use of taxes rather than general revenues to compute the effort index; and (2) double-counting of state-local income taxes. Table 4, therefore, shows the percentage changes produced in each state area grant by implementing either of those seemingly minor variations.

Column 7 of Table 2 reflects a different effort formula, that in which revenues rather than population are weighted by the effort index. This formula is used in the Mills bill to determine roughly half of the distribution to state governments. The other half of the Mills allocation to state governments is based primarily on state personal income tax collections, as described in earlier chapters. The results of this formula appear in column 8 and, finally, the overall state government results under the Mills bill are indicated in column 9.

---

[4] The exact formula is:

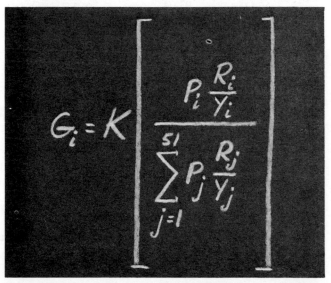

$$G_i = K \left[\frac{P_i \frac{R_i}{Y_i}}{\sum_{j=1}^{51} P_j \frac{R_j}{Y_j}} \right]$$

where R is state-local revenues and the other variables have the same significance as in note 2 in this chapter.

TABLE 3   LOCAL GOVERNMENT GRANTS UNDER MILLS PLAN AS % OF GRANTS UNDER STRAIGHT POPULATION FORMULA

(1969-70 Averages)

	Percent		*Percent*
ALABAMA	99.41	NEBRASKA	90.03
ALASKA	61.60	NEVADA	100.65
ARIZONA	106.82	NEW HAMPSHIRE	82.38
ARKANSAS	90.43	NEW JERSEY	109.72
CALIFORNIA	108.26	NEW MEXICO	91.45
COLORADO	104.24	NEW YORK	104.90
CONNECTICUT	99.22	NORTH CAROLINA	86.89
DELAWARE	99.25	NORTH DAKOTA	79.56
FLORIDA	103.63	OHIO	100.91
GEORGIA	95.06	OKLAHOMA	95.53
HAWAII	95.47	OREGON	94.69
IDAHO	77.64	PENNSYLVANIA	99.48
ILLINOIS	102.08	RHODE ISLAND	110.84
INDIANA	93.04	SOUTH CAROLINA	91.26
IOWA	84.78	SOUTH DAKOTA	79.96
KANSAS	86.57	TENNESSEE	96.59
KENTUCKY	94.92	TEXAS	105.04
LOUISIANA	101.80	UTAH	112.94
MAINE	83.59	VERMONT	70.60
MARYLAND	101.25	VIRGINIA	98.42
MASSACHUSETTS	106.47	WASHINGTON	96.26
MICHIGAN	100.65	WEST VIRGINIA	87.33
MINNESOTA	95.51	WISCONSIN	94.52
MISSISSIPPI	91.24	WYOMING	70.01
MISSOURI	99.44	DISTRICT OF	
MONTANA	83.03	COLUMBIA	119.22

Average Deviation from Population Grant ±5.4%

TABLE 4   PERCENTAGE OF CHANGES IN STATE AREA GRANTS FOR MODIFICATIONS OF ADMINISTRATION BILL

(Based on 1969-70 Two-Year Average)

	Effort Based on Taxes Instead of Gen'l Revenue	*Double-Counting of Income Taxes*
ALABAMA	−11.55	− 0.87
ALASKA	−76.22	17.74
ARIZONA	− 0.79	− 1.48
ARKANSAS	− 5.77	− 1.88
CALIFORNIA	2.41	− 0.32
COLORADO	− 3.06	3.79
CONNECTICUT	6.92	− 9.80
DELAWARE	− 8.23	19.40
FLORIDA	− 4.38	−10.32
GEORGIA	− 7.07	2.11
HAWAII	3.07	13.87
IDAHO	− 2.07	6.67
ILLINOIS	7.09	2.38
INDIANA	− 2.03	0.65
IOWA	0.44	− 1.44
KANSAS	− 3.86	− 1.68
KENTUCKY	− 3.97	1.92
LOUISIANA	− 9.84	− 5.38
MAINE	6.31	− 4.67
MARYLAND	3.37	11.46
MASSACHUSETTS	9.61	8.09
MICHIGAN	0.01	− 0.08
MINNESOTA	− 3.37	9.89
MISSISSIPPI	− 5.69	− 3.70
MISSOURI	0.52	− 2.23
MONTANA	− 1.58	3.71
NEBRASKA	− 5.33	− 2.42
NEVADA	− 6.27	−10.32

(continued)

58

Table 4 continued

	Effort Based on Taxes Instead of Gen'l Revenue	Double-Counting of Income Taxes
NEW HAMPSHIRE	2.16	− 8.64
NEW JERSEY	6.69	− 9.77
NEW MEXICO	−13.89	− 0.92
NEW YORK	6.44	0.89
NORTH CAROLINA	− 0.84	7.27
NORTH DAKOTA	−16.63	− 3.74
OHIO	− 2.32	−10.32
OKLAHOMA	−10.27	− 3.63
OREGON	− 4.44	13.96
PENNSYLVANIA	6.09	− 9.02
RHODE ISLAND	7.16	− 3.56
SOUTH CAROLINA	− 2.58	3.60
SOUTH DAKOTA	− 2.77	−10.32
TENNESSEE	− 3.05	− 9.27
TEXAS	− 5.08	−10.32
UTAH	− 2.93	4.73
VERMONT	6.33	10.41
VIRGINIA	1.27	7.20
WASHINGTON	− 5.15	−10.32
WEST VIRGINIA	− 0.09	− 1.58
WISCONSIN	3.86	11.59
WYOMING	−14.99	−10.32
DISTRICT OF COLUMBIA	10.07	−10.32

It is, of course, impossible to illustrate all of the alternative plans, since there are clearly innumerable ways of combining even the few major formula principles underlying Table 2. Also, even a variation in the "weights" given to the formulas will produce important changes in a plan which, like the Mills bill, combines several different distributional principles. Nonetheless, it is interesting to note the great variance in the results depicted in Table 2, especially since each of the principles reflected have, at one time or another, commanded considerable support in the revenue-sharing debate. This bears out the opening suggestion of this study that the broad concept of revenue sharing encompasses many plans which differ substantially in their underlying principles. Moreover, the political popularity of the various alternatives may in the future display swings as wide and as sudden as some of those already experienced, thus leading to radical alternatives in the concepts underlying any existing legislation.

It is also worth noting that the Table 2 results do not reflect the impact of incentive effect features which, as was discussed in Chapter III, are present in some of the formulas. Thus, five years after the implementation of revenue sharing, some of these results may differ considerably. Still, the illustrative results do permit one to gain some quantitative feel for the distributional implications of various revenue-sharing options.

INTRASTATE EFFECTS

Besides the redistributive effects among state areas, the similar effects among government units *within* states are also of interest.

The 1971 administration bill proposed allocating all grants within a state area on the collection basis, i.e., in proportion to the revenues raised by the various governments. This formula mitigates the apparent redistributiveness of the interstate allocations, since it generally allots higher per capita grants to higher income government units. (Per capita revenues of local units tend to vary directly with income.) Variations on this bill included the Muskie bill which modified the basic collection-based grant by a "poverty factor" determined by a unit's relative proportion of low income families and families receiving government assistance. Other variations included an adjustment to favor larger-sized government units, especially large urban centers. However, even without the difficult-to-justify formulas which adjust for local government size, a collection-based system would, on the average, result in substantially higher per capita disbursements to large cities than to small ones. For instance, in recent years the per capita revenues of cities over 1 million have been more than triple those of cities less than 50,000, and this fact would be directly convertible into proportionate differences in their per capita receipts under a collection-based formula.

Under the original provisions of the Mills bill, the allocation among local governments within each state might actually tend to be slightly *more* redistributive than the interstate allocations indicate. The same principles of population, urban population, and inverse per capita income are used to distribute grants among county areas. However, the split-ups to lower-level governments then drop the urbanized population criterion. Since urbanization is correlated with relatively high income, this removes what may be regarded as an antiredistributive element in the grant allocation formulas. On the other hand, the Mills plan gives states the option to substitute population weighted by per capita taxes for the straight population principle at all levels of the intrastate distribution. Since per capita taxes are higher in high-income areas, the exercise of this option would diminish the redistributiveness of the grant allocations.

REDISTRIBUTION TO GOVERNMENTS RATHER THAN PEOPLE

The figures previously presented in Tables 2, 3, and 4 necessarily describe redistribution in terms of political units and geographic areas. This is so because the recipients of the grants are governments and not individuals. If we are interested in revenue sharing's redistributive impact on *people*, the argument must be traced a step further. In particular, there is some possibility that any equalizing effects among broad geographic areas may be at least partially offset by the income-class benefits which revenue sharing generates as the state-local sector adjusts to these new funds. Although we know that recipient governments must spread revenue-sharing funds over the options of tax-cutting and expenditure, the specific manner in which they do so affects the degree of redistribution which takes place among individual citizens.

One way of estimating how state-local units will spend revenue-sharing grants is to extrapolate, on a function-by-function basis, their previous marginal propensities for spending new revenues.[5] State-local governments always tend to allocate over 50 percent of new revenues to education,[6] but significant state-to-state differences exist in other program areas. An analysis by Weidenbaum suggests that the ratio of people-oriented expenditures (such as health, welfare, etc.) to physical capital expenditures (such as highways and natural resources) may be inversely related to the interstate redistributiveness of the different revenue-sharing formulas. If the benefits of the lower income classes are more heavily affected by the former types of expenditures, then geographic redistribution might be

[5] An extrapolation of this type was performed by James L. Plummer, "Federal-State Revenue Sharing," *Southern Economic Journal*, (July 1966), 122–24.

[6] While education is not included in the "high priority" local government expenditures prescribed in the Mills bill, the reader should recall the Chapter I argument that "money mixes" and makes such broad categorical restrictions ineffective in practice. It is not clear what effect (if any) on state-local education expenditure propensities will occur because of the recent court decisions on school finances.

dampened by a contrary income-class effect.[7] Thus, one can only speculate about the income-class allocation of benefits from new grants-stimulated state-local expenditures.

Conclusions on the *tax* side likewise depend on what one regards as the "marginal" tax provisions which state-local governments will adjust in response to the revenue-sharing grants. It is argued by some that revenue sharing should replace the funds generated by regressive and dis-tributionally "inferior" state-local revenue systems with the "superior" funds from the progressive federal income tax. Viewed from this standpoint, it makes a substantial difference whether the state-local taxes replaced come from income taxes, sales taxes, property taxes, or excise taxes. When the revenue-sharing legislation contains incentives for the use of income taxes, it becomes less likely that any "replacement" effect will fall upon state or local income taxes.

An attempt to accomplish redistribution by general purpose payments to governments is a rather peculiar tool. There is no reliable means of predicting the manner in which the recipient governments will pass on the resultant benefits to individual citizens or what the income-class pattern of these benefits will be.

MEASURING NEED, EFFORT, AND CAPACITY

Thus far, redistribution has been discussed as if income levels were, in themselves, valid criteria by which "need" should be judged. But in the plans which have gained popular support, "need" in a more extended sense also

---

[7] Murray L. Weidenbaum, "Federal Aid to State and Local Governments: The Policy Alternatives," in *Revenue Sharing and Its Alternatives*, Hearings of the Joint Economic Committee (Washington, D.C.: U.S. Government Printing Office, 1967), esp. pp. 658–59.

seems to be implied by the introduction of measures of *fiscal capacity* such as the "effort index."

In this connection, the Advisory Commission on Intergovernmental Relations issued a report which surveys various measures of fiscal capacity and divides them into two basic forms: (1) the tax source or income approach, and (2) the tax base or representative tax system approach.[8] The personal income figures used in the various revenue-sharing plans reflect only income *received* in a state and not income *produced* in a state, although the latter may be a significant source of tax receipts. The Plains, Rocky Mountain, and Southwestern states generally rank higher in income produced than income received, while the opposite is true of the New England and Midwestern regions. Thus, a more sophisticated basis for measuring fiscal capacity might alter the revenue-sharing distributions between regions.[9]

In connection with the efficiency discussion in Chapter II, tax burden was described in terms of *rates*. The second category of capacity measurement is akin to this. The bases available for taxation are examined in each state and then the amounts of revenue generated by a uniform tax system are also estimated on a state-by-state basis. These benchmark revenue collections are used to measure relative fiscal capacity. Such measures of "need" do not appear to have been seriously considered in the revenue-sharing discussions.

Besides the objections which can be levied against the various indices of fiscal capacity, the use of population as the implicit expenditure "need" index is also highly questionable. Many persons concerned about the potential of revenue sharing for redressing distributional inequities might find it more appealing to base revenue-sharing

[8] *Measuring the Fiscal Capacity and Effect of State and Local Areas* (A.C.I.R., Washington, D.C., 1971).

[9] A fairly detailed discussion of the revenue-sharing implications of different effort measures may be found in Allen D. Manvel, "Differences in Fiscal Capacity and Effort: Their Significance for a Federal Revenue Sharing System," *National Tax Journal*, 24 (June 1971), 193–204.

transfers on an explicit effort to calculate the *gap* between a state's capacity and its need. Musgrave and Polinsky have attempted at least a rough estimate of such gaps, using a representative tax system and the per capita costs to provide a standard of output or performance.[10]

Suppose we then judge revenue-sharing plans by their relative ability to absorb the calculated deficiencies or gaps. The results do not always correlate well with measures of the redistributiveness, narrowly defined, of the alternative plans. The per capita formula, for instance, performs better than the more redistributive effort-based formula of the 1971 administration bill. But the third example analyzed by Musgrave and Polinsky, the Javits plan, ranks best of all. This latter is also the most redistributive, being essentially a combination of a 15 percent inverse income and an 85 percent effort-weighted population distribution. Thus, it would be visionary to expect that simple redistributiveness is a reliable guide to the extent by which alternative revenue-sharing plans meet more sophisticated measures of fiscal "need."

It is worth noting parenthetically that transfers based on a concept similar to the Musgrave-Polinsky gaps would have none of the types of incentive effects discussed in Chapter III, since the representative tax system and the output standards are hypothetical measurements only; the state's *actual* fiscal behavior has no effect. Whether this is good or bad depends, of course, on how one feels about the incentives in the other formulas.

In sum, if the way is laid open to making value judgments about "what should be done," the popular measures of income and "effort" should hardly be regarded as having a lock on all of the good arguments. What they do have, though, is a conceptual simplicity which has apparently had strong intuitive appeal.

---

[10] Richard A. Musgrave and A. Mitchell Polinsky, "Revenue Sharing—A Critical View," in *Financing State and Local Governments* (Federal Reserve Bank of Boston, 1970), pp. 17–52.

WHO BENEFITS?

Only the naive and unworldly would leave a discussion of distribution effects entirely on an altruistic plane. The level of awareness about revenue-sharing provisions and the tactical advantages or disadvantages they imply for certain political units is probably still low, even after more than ten years of discussion. If and when the situation changes, one would expect it to have considerable influence on the evolution of the legislation. An example may be helpful. Based on pure matters of principle, the "taxes versus general revenues" argument on revenue eligibility seems reasonably well balanced. A politician could easily be expected to support the form of legislation which most benefits his own constituency.

Thus far, there is remarkably little evidence of parochialism in the attitudes of politicians toward revenue sharing. There has been a tendency to support or oppose the general concept without asking "*Which* revenue sharing?" One can only wonder how far revenue sharing's support might decline if the interunit distributional implications of the enacted plan and of alternatives to it were faced more squarely.

V
IMPACT ON THE FEDERAL SYSTEM

We have already surveyed the redistributive aspects of revenue sharing which are likely to play a large role in the assessment of revenue sharing by a fiscal "liberal." The "strengthening and rehabilitation of our federal system" has also been a prominent note in the debate. For some, revenue sharing's impact on fiscal federalism surely is only a subsidiary consideration relative to other possible goals cited earlier. For many others, however, strengthening the position of the states vis-à-vis that of the federal government is *the* paramount issue. This latter group sees revenue sharing as the tool by which the whole future structure of the federal system can be altered in favor of a more independent and vigorous role for the states. The desirability of such a result is, for purposes of argument, accepted as a premise in this chapter. Concern will be focused almost exclusively on whether revenue sharing can be expected to have the anticipated effect either as to direction or as to strength.

The proposition that revenue sharing will truly strengthen and help the states has strong intuitive appeal and seems to speak for itself. It is the possible negative case which, in the interests of a balanced debate, needs to be set out more carefully. In this case, the discussion in these pages deliberately exhibits a bias in the attention it gives to potential negative factors about the effect of revenue sharing on the federal system.

"SPECIAL REVENUE SHARING"

The debate about *general* revenue sharing has been needlessly confused by arguments which apply principally to the so-called "special revenue sharing." The latter is essentially a reform and regrouping of the numerous and hideously complicated categorical grant programs into six general functional areas: rural community development, urban community development, manpower, education, law enforcement, and transportation. Grants-in-aid would be distributed to local governments on the basis of broad formulas which attempt to reflect need. The major difference between this and the existing categorical grants is that it would allegedly be less piecemeal, more subject to rational review and control, and not as sensitive to grantsmanship. As in the past, however, the basic principles of matching payments, project-area specification, and some general performance standards would presumably be maintained.

Reform of the categorical grants would certainly increase the ability of state-local units to coordinate their spending, even on externality-producing public goods, without unwarranted and unproductive federal restrictions. However, the basic conditional, special-purpose nature of these grants sets them apart from the general-purpose funds of the type envisioned in regular revenue sharing. In sum, it may be well to loosen some of the superfluous strings and complexities of the categorical grants, but this is an issue quite independent of revenue sharing properly defined.

THE LURKING QUID PRO QUO

A glance at the political history of the development of revenue-sharing proposals should make partisans of the states' independence a bit nervous. In the basic formulas, we see a progression from the collection-based tax-sharing notion to increasingly complex formulas which frequently include incentive devices such as effort indexes. Mandatory pass-through emerges. Implicit and explicit incentives for particular tax forms and particular local government structures appear. To establish eligibility, governors are asked to submit plans and timetables for various reforms deemed desirable by congressmen. Although the enacted revenue-sharing bill does omit some of these provisions, it is not at all necessarily immune to them.

One can hardly be surprised that he who has something valuable to give will learn to ask for something in return. When there exists a genuine exchange relationship between two parties, there is nothing strange about the existence of a *quid pro quo* arrangement. Exactly who is exchanging with whom is not obvious in the present context, however. A cynic may wonder why a voter's federal representative should be "bribing" his state representative to do something that the state representative thinks the voter would not want done. To the extent that the revenue-sharing proposals incorporate value judgments, this latter view suggests that a dominant federal coalition may use revenue sharing as a means of accommodating state-local decisions to national norms. One may argue that such interference is good, at least in certain instances, but it can hardly be equated with enlarging the degree of independence and diversity in a federal system.

The history of state grants to localities provides some insight in this general question. In a number of states, aid to local schools originated as a fairly broad form of tax sharing (of the property tax), but developed over time into highly conditional grants involving a great deal of higher-level control. The pressures for such evolution are strong and, in the case of revenue sharing, the process was already apparent even before any legislation had been enacted into law.

PROGNOSIS FOR CHANGE

Hopefully, the preceding chapters have already belied the frequently-heard sentiment that the various alternative revenue-sharing proposals are "different in detail, but basically similar in principle." In some cases, superficially innocuous "details" can have powerful effects. In other cases, to accept a "mild" application of a principle makes it difficult to argue against "more effective" applications of the same principle at a later date. Revenue-sharing bills abound with such examples.

An ardent states' rights partisan may, for instance, already mildly object to some of the weighting schemes in the distributional formulas. But if income taxes are to be double-weighted, why not triple? If states should be rewarded in proportion to "effort," why not at an exponential rather than a linear rate? (The National League of Cities benchmark-effect device is already a step in this direction.) If some taxes are to be supereligible, why not make certain others *in*eligible, perhaps because they are "regressive"? Particularly in light of the analysis in Chapter III, the incentive effects of these potential changes can be surprisingly powerful. Yet, all they represent is an extension of principles which already command widespread political support and which have generated relatively little controversy.

The potential impact of other eligibility requirements is perhaps equally as great as the potential consequences of formula gamesmanship. When the proposed requirement for a master plan to be filed by state governors was described earlier, the absence of any enforcement provision was noted. In any event, many people would agree with the general spirit of most, if not all, of the specific reforms mentioned. Nevertheless, if such provisions were to be made *effective*, as they certainly can be, would the state-independence advocates feel comfortable about each state's annual "plan" having to pass federal review before revenue-sharing funds can be received?

INDEPENDENCE SOLD CHEAPLY

At minimum, the possibilities raised above should generate some uneasiness, even if they are viewed as somewhat alarmist. This uneasiness cannot be laid to rest merely by admitting that he who pays the piper gets (sooner or later) to call the tune. Under revenue sharing, after all, the federal government does not propose to pay a very significant share of the piper's bill. Whatever independence the states surrender in accepting the present *categorical* grants is at least sold at reasonably high rates; federal money accounts for better than $1 out of every $6 of state-local general revenues. Although the impact of any incentive provisions attached to revenue sharing would obviously vary to some extent with the size of the total distribution, realistic analysis suggests that the effects might be significant even with a total disbursement of as little as $5 billion, which is only about 3 percent of the total state-local revenues.

Revenue sharing can produce large behavioral effects with relatively small sums because it pays grants to lower-level units based on their relative rather than their absolute behavior. The revenue-sharing formulas focus their effect at the decision-making margin and place states and local units in competition with one another. For instance, suppose that all states were to respond to the effort incentive by raising their taxes by the same proportionate amount. In contrast to the categorical grants, where such behavior is genuinely "rewarded," each state would find itself with precisely the same revenue-sharing entitlement as before.

Thus, increasing federally desirable behavior in this zero-sum competitive game context can be accomplished by the national government with unusual effectiveness.

Like the proverbial mess of pottage, revenue sharing may thus be viewed by a skeptic as a comparatively small compensation for what is surrendered.

SECTOR SIZE CONSIDERATIONS

New Federalism has become a rallying cry for opponents of "big government." Of course, such opponents bemoan the rate of growth in the absolute size of the public sector. But they also tend to be powerfully concerned with the division of responsibilities within the government sector, preferring to see the role of state-local government strengthened relative to the federal government. This group thus provides a sizeable fraction of the support for revenue sharing.

If the marginal subsidy rates presented in Chapter III were fully understood, it is difficult to see why opponents of "excessive" government growth would find the effort-weighted formulas acceptable. Demand analysis suggests that dollars transferred out of the federal public goods sector and into revenue sharing will increase the total size of the combined federal-state-local public sector, possibly by a substantial multiple. The following analysis, while certainly oversimplified, indicates the general forces in play.

Suppose that $1 billion is transferred out of the federal sector via revenue sharing. This sum would represent less than a one percent *average* subsidy on state-local purchases. Hence, an expansion of only one percent in the quantity of state-local services demanded would overcompensate the federal budget decrease and actually enlarge the size of the total public sector. If the $1 billion of revenue-sharing funds is distributed through one of the formulas which contains the lower-level government's tax effort as a determinant, then it may plausibly be argued that the expected increase in demand for state-local public goods will indeed amount to more than 1 percent. As indicated in Chapter III, the *marginal* price reduction caused by $1 billion in revenue-sharing funds tends to be substantially higher than 1 percent. In order for these incentive formulas not to generate a net increase in public sector size, the demand for state-local public goods would have to be well down into the price-insensitive range of what economists call "inelastic" demand.[1]

To a public sector expansionist, the above should be good news. More fiscally "conservative" individuals will probably view the conclusion with some dismay. They must ask whether it is really desirable to decrease the federal public sector by $1 billion at the cost of increasing another (even if "preferable") area of the public sector by some multiple of $1 billion.

OTHER "CONSERVATIVE" CONCERNS

The role of political philosophy in judging whether revenue sharing is desirable suggests one final observation about possible effects on the balance of executive-legislative power. Suggestions have been made that control of funds from revenue sharing would increase the relative power of mayors and governors; however, it is not immediately clear

---

[1] For more technically minded readers, it should be observed that the usual notion of price elasticity does not apply strictly here. The price decrease is heavier at the margin than it is inframarginally, so that the income effect is less strong than in the ordinary case. However, the marginal substitution effect should alone support the general line of reasoning in the text.

how the executive branches would "control" these monies any more than those from, say, sales taxes. Presumably, revenue-sharing funds would be subject to legislative appropriation just as would any other revenue source. Nor is it easy to see why the "trust fund" nature of the federal allotment would, as alleged, shift power from Congress to the executive branch. Since the level and disposition of the funds has been prestipulated by Congress, the executive branch would exercise an exclusively administrative role.

The exception to this could occur at the federal level if, for instance, a suitable "annual plan" really were required of each state. Even if Congress set guidelines for the suitability of such plans, it is inevitable that considerable discretion would be exercised by the executive branch in its practical interpretation of the rules.

THE CARROT AND THE STICK

Folklore is full of stories about flies being caught with honey and about carrots versus sticks. What has been suggested here is that any grant will, sooner or later, be used as a carrot and that carrots are, behaviorally speaking, really just a civilized form of stick. People who think revenue sharing promises an improvement in the present trend of public sector size and organization would do well to examine the issues more carefully. Perhaps revenue sharing is all that they hope it is. And perhaps it isn't!

VI
WHERE DO WE STAND?

Chapter I commenced with the assertion that "the discussion of revenue sharing has been characterized by an extraordinary amount of confusion as to what revenue sharing actually entails in practice and what it is supposed to accomplish." Hopefully, the reasons for such confusion have become somewhat more apparent in the intervening pages.

AMBIGUITIES AND CONTRADICTIONS

On the one hand, little consideration has been given to the effects of provisions which are thought to entail only minor variations in the legislation but which have far-reaching potential impact on the structure of fiscal federalism in the United States. In some cases, this impact is primarily one of different interstate revenue distributions, but in other cases the provisions substantially alter the behavioral incentives within the state-local sector. While choice among these alternatives must ultimately be dictated by one's own subjective value judgments or political philosophy, it seems absurd that the differences between the alternative forms of revenue sharing have widely been regarded as relatively trivial. If and when the consequences of the various revenue-sharing plans come into clearer focus, the existing support for the concept is almost certain to weaken.

On the other hand, the vague conception of what revenue sharing entails is matched by equally amorphous —and sometimes contradictory—notions about its expected or desired effects. For instance, the substitution of progressive federal finances for relatively regressive state-local taxes is viewed by many as a notable objective of revenue sharing. However, the incorporation of an effort index in the distribution formulas appears to promote the goal of expanded state-local public sectors precisely by discouraging the substitution of federal monies for state-local taxes. Also, fiscal conservatives frankly see the curtailment of the federal categorical grant program as an important by-product of revenue sharing, while the more liberal public sector activists visualize the new grant program as merely complementary to the existing system. This illustrates how the various proponents of revenue sharing frequently argue from inconsistent assumptions about the reactions of federal, state, and local politicians to the existence of a revenue-sharing system. Henry Aaron subscribes to a quite similar view when he assesses the causes for the inconclusive nature of the revenue-sharing debate:

> The first reason is that contradictory assumptions about the consequences of revenue sharing are implicit in the list of objectives revenue sharing is supposed to advance. The second is that neither economists nor political scientists can answer the crucial economic and political questions about the consequences of revenue sharing.[1]

Such observations do not paint a flattering picture of the decision-making process out of which the current revenue-sharing bills have emerged.

---

[1] Henry Aaron, "The Honest Citizen's Guide to Revenue Sharing," in *Proceedings* of the 1971 meeting of the National Tax Association (forthcoming).

WISHING DOESN'T MAKE IT TRUE

A dispassionate reader will probably not gather much enthusiasm for revenue sharing from the discussion presented in the previous chapters. Notwithstanding the fervent rhetoric on the subject, it is by no means clear that revenue sharing, at least as presently conceived, possesses curative powers for any objectively identifiable efficiency problem in the state-local public sector. Indeed, it is legitimate to ask whether some of the incentive effects generated by revenue sharing are not excessive or even counterproductive.

A willingness to enter the more value-laden area of redistribution still does not make a strong case for revenue sharing. At best, transfers to state-local governments appear to be relatively clumsy tools for attacking low income problems. There are also a host of other problems even with accurately assessing the redistributive impact of the various plans. Considering the possible alternative uses of the funds, the attractiveness of revenue sharing to fiscal liberals is difficult to defend.

But it is undoubtedly among the fiscally conservative that revenue sharing has received the most uncritical acceptance. Conservatives see the plan as a damper on both the growth of federal spending and on federal control as exerted through the "strings" of categorical grant programs. However, they have largely ignored the ability of federal legislators to impose conditions and formulas capable of inducing the states to modify their behavior in accord with federal goals. Contrary to the popular rhetoric, a defensible argument can be made that revenue sharing will ultimately develop along lines which will curtail rather than expand the independence of the states.

Finally, there is the attitude of the typical voter, the proverbial man on the streetcorner. It is understandable

but unfortunate that he would like to believe in revenue-sharing funds as akin to manna from heaven. This flies in the face of the inescapable fact that, on the average, revenue sharing is equivalent to passing a taxpayer's own money from one pocket to the other.

In sum, when all the fanfares die away, revenue sharing stands bereft of any real fiscal magic. That does not imply that it should be rejected out of hand. In principle, there may well be forms of revenue sharing which would command an enthusiastic consensus from informed persons. Nevertheless, a close examination of the debate which has led to the present legislation reveals a startling superficiality and immaturity.

Suppose that revenue sharing does have a really major potential significance for the future of fiscal federalism in America. Should we continue to support its enactment even despite the confusion and illusion which characterize the public debate? In the face of no strong objective arguments for revenue sharing and a host of uncertainties about its precise form and consequences, an affirmative vote for revenue sharing is not easy to justify.

$1.95

Rather than a source of vital fiscal assistance, will revenue sharing turn out to be merely a clumsy fiscal instrument that doesn't do anything well? Since it was first proposed in the 1950s, the idea of revenue sharing has had many adherents with varied and sometimes contradictory notions of what it means, and what it is intended to accomplish. And as a policy has taken shape, too little critical attention has focused on the impact that specific provisions can be expected to have on federal-state-local fiscal relationships. Consequently Charles Goetz predicts that revenue sharing, in practice, may surprise and disappoint many of its supporters.

The purpose of this monograph is to examine what is meant by revenue sharing, and to suggest some of the implications of various revenue-sharing proposals. Although the book was initiated during a period of intense debate on the subject and its publication nearly coincides with the enactment of a compromise bill, the author's intention is not to report on this legislation. Rather, the book is written with the assumption that interest in revenue sharing will increase, especially as we begin to find out how it works in actual practice. It is hoped, therefore, that this book will contribute to further debate, appraisal, and clarification.

Charles J. Goetz is professor of economics at the Center for the Study of Public Choice, Virginia Polytechnic Institute and University.

The Urban Institute
2100 M Street, N.W.,, Washington, D.C. 20037